LETTERS FROM SACHIKO

LETTERS FROM SACHIKO

A Japanese Woman's View of Life in the Land of the Economic Miracle

JAMES TRAGER

Atheneum

NEW YORK   1982

Copyright © 1982 by James Trager

Library of Congress Cataloging in Publication Data

Trager, James.
  Letters from Sachiko.

    Includes index.

    1. Japan—Social conditions—1945-   —Addresses,
essays, lectures. 2. Women—Japan—Social conditions—
Addresses, essays, lectures. I. Title.
HN723.5.T7 1982   306'.0952   82-45312
ISBN 0-689-11337-4   AACR2

Editorial, Graphics and Production by Cobb/Dunlop, Inc.

Published simultaneously in Canada by McClelland and Stewart Ltd.
Manufactured by The Maple-Vail Company, Manchester, Penna.
First Edition

For
"Dear Chie" with affectionate admiration.
A deep bow, also, to Ken Hirata,
and another to Goro Kuramochi.

INTRODUCTION

My wife Chie Nishio, the photographer I met in Bucharest in the summer of 1969, has seen her native Japan emerge from starvation and defeat in 1945 to become an economic power in many ways second only to the United States. Since coming to America, she has watched this country try, under four presidents, to deal with its "malaise," as one president called it, and regain the economic momentum it once had.

Looking at one's own country through the eyes of a foreigner gives one a new perspective on matters that never before seemed to require examination. If the foreigner is from a country with more than half the population of the United States but less than four percent of this country's land and virtually no natural resources, some obvious questions arise. How is it possible that Japan can outdo the United States in producing automobiles, steel, ships, motorbikes, bicycles, television sets, tape recorders, transistor radios, stereo equipment, cameras, binoculars, wristwatches, and pocket calculators? Even the bats and gloves used in the Great American Pastime are now made in Japan (although the mountain ash for the bats may come from Louisville, Kentucky, and the leather for the gloves from Texas). How did "Made in Japan" change from being a mark of shoddy goods to a sign of quality? (Products made in Taiwan and elsewhere now sometimes sport bogus "Made in Japan" labels.) What are the Japanese doing right that we are doing wrong? And what is it like for a woman to live in the country that is so envied by so much of the world?

This book provides some new insights into what Japan is doing right. As to the question of women's life in Japan, the answers came straight from the source—in the form of letters to Chie from a younger sister back home.

"Sachiko Shimada"* is actually a composite. Chie and her sisters were all born in Yonago, a small city in Tottori Prefecture on the Sea of Japan. "Sachiko" and her husband Toshiro now live in Omiya City on the outskirts of Tokyo, as do her sisters Tamiko and Yoko (all the names have been changed, and certain details have been altered, to protect the privacy of those concerned). The Shimadas' son Hajime is in elementary school. In addition to their insights into what the Japanese are doing right, Sachiko's letters and the supplementary material in this book may prompt readers to rethink some of the common misconceptions about the status of women in modern Japan—false ideas based on the Madame Butterfly stereotype.

The letters speak for themselves. I have begun each one with "Dear Chie" in deference to Western ideas as to how a letter should open; it is not customary for a Japanese letter to begin with any salutation. Except for bracketed [ ] translations of words or phrases and conversions from Japanese or metric measures, my own comments are in the notes at the back of the book, placed there so as not to intrude. These notes are based in part on several visits to Japan and in part on material translated for me by Chie. They explain Japanese words, point out things the reader might not otherwise notice or find significant, and give some background information. Ruth Benedict, the late American cultural anthropologist whose classic study of Japanese society (*The Chrysanthemum and the Sword*) appeared after World War II, had never set foot in Japan, so I make no apology for having only limited direct knowledge of my wife's native land. Note 45 has special interest for readers seeking answers to why it costs Detroit seventeen hundred dollars more to produce a small, well-built automobile than it costs Toyota, Nissan, Honda, Subaru, or Toyo Kogyo (Mazda).

*Shimada Sachiko in the Japanese style. All names in this book are in the Western style, with given names first.

Robert S. Ozaki wrote in his 1978 book *The Japanese, A Cultural Portrait:*

"Since there must be some relief for Japanese men who struggle in the chilly waters of human relations, many Japanese women, after growing up, remain babyish, sweet-voiced, soft-mannered, delicate, and doll-like; girls whose inborn personalities are of the opposite kind try or pretend to be so. This is their subconscious response to the need of Japanese men who, in their mature years, retain their mother-complexes and seek spiritual as well as physical comfort in playing the baby to their women."

"Sachiko" may play the role of comforter in her marriage and on the surface conform to Ozaki's stereotype; yet her letters are perfectly straightforward in dealing with everyday riddles that puzzle some Americans: Why do women who protest so much about their lack of equal rights continue to play by men's rules? Why don't more women get their acts together and make their own careers? Can a woman not be successful in her own right as an entrepreneur, physician, lawyer, politician, engineer, teacher, writer, artist, or whatever? If women really want to get more out of life, what is stopping them? Are the obstacles placed before them really any worse than those that confront many men?

While Sachiko does not pretend to have all the answers, at least she focuses in her own way on the right questions. Her solutions, often silky and subtle, are not in the least inscrutable. Some readers, in fact, may find Sachiko's clear-eyed ideas useful in their own lives, wherever they may be, whatever their circumstances.

桜の花も　やわらかな春の日差しのなかで可愛ら

しい蕾をすこしずつふくらませて参りました。

眠りはニューヨークからのお便り嬉しく拝見

致しました。

Dear Chie,

Your letter arrived yesterday and I was happy to hear from you. Your visit here was all too short after so long an absence, and we enjoyed meeting James-san, about whom we had heard so much. I trust the Food and Agriculture people in Rome were pleased by your report of what you had accomplished with the farmers' cooperatives in South Korea.

As we discussed while you were here, everybody is still embarrassed about the Lockheed scandal. After nearly two years, the courtroom proceedings against Tanaka-san [former prime minister Kakuei Tanaka] still drag on, and although it seems quite clear that he accepted nearly four hundred and forty million yen [about two million two hundred thousand dollars], he remains popular and very powerful. Some people say Tanaka-san took the money for the good of the country, and maybe they even believe it. There is nevertheless a lot of distrust, not only of cabinet ministers and Diet members but also of big business and higher-ups in the government. People are cynical, I'm afraid, and that is in many ways the most unfortunate aspect of the situation. Our senator, Fusae Ichikawa, is still going strong at age eighty-six and I am so proud to have a woman like that in office (1). She is as outspoken as ever and has more integrity than any other politician I know; she makes the men look crooked, even when they are not. If ever there were an example of how using the head and body continuously keeps one young, she is that; I hope I age as beautifully as she has. As a member of the *Sangiin* [upper house of the Diet] she has far less power, of course, than someone in the *Shugiin* [lower house], but at least her voice gets heard. She does not belong to any party, and in the *Shugiin* an individual member's vote counts for very little. Everybody in the *Shugiin* has to follow the party policy. They have elected quite a few people, including women, to the *Sangiin* who are not really qualified but are merely well-known through having written books or having appeared on television. The people who really hold power are all men and they get themselves reelected time after time, scandal or no scandal.

It is hard for me to believe that we women have been permitted to vote only since 1946. So much has changed for women here since the war, yet I wonder if most of us do not still live as if things were still the same, with only men able to vote, or hold office, or own property (2).

The woman down the hall told me this morning that she had spent the whole afternoon yesterday in a *pachinko* parlor (3). She went on and on about how she had won some cans of cling peaches and I had to think to myself that there must be some more constructive way for her to spend her time, although I don't mean to pass judgment on her, and I have to ask myself, after all, what am I really doing with my own time?

Speaking of time, Kazuko Fukuda (that's my neighbor's name) did tell me one thing I found interesting, although it may not be anything new to my big sister in America. It's about feminine hygiene. I was having my period and feeling pretty bad. She noticed, and she said the average woman feels uncomfortable six days out of every month. Then she told me about a kind of cleansing douche that reduces the period of discomfort to three days. That adds up to thirty-six days a year, she reminded me, and I am really quite curious to try it. Do you know anything about this?

Sachiko

◌6

25 March

Dear Chie,

A friend and I were having American coffee in the lounge of the Mitsui Building overlooking Shinjuku yesterday, and I was astonished to see how much the city has changed in the last few years. So many new buildings have gone up that you would not recognize it, and they are still building more. The new buildings are not very attractive, I'm afraid. With space so valuable, I should think they would try harder to make each building spectacularly tasteful. Instead, the new Supreme Court building is quite ugly, as are many others.

Oto-o-san [Father] is nearly eighty, you know, yet he remains in good shape. He came to visit us last month, as I may have written you. It was his first visit since 1973, when he received that Zuihosho medal (4) from the Emperor at the Imperial Palace, and he could hardly believe that they had put up so many tall buildings in Tokyo. We took him and *Oka-a-san* [Mother] to the top of the new International Trade Center building at Hamamatsu-cho Station where the monorail leaves for Haneda Airport, and the view from the fortieth floor there is breathtaking. It was a clear day and we could see Fuji-san in the distance. It was quite majestic, although really no more impressive, I think, than Daisen [the mountain that looms over Yonago].

Oto-o-san and *Oka-a-san* are so sweet together. They are a lovely old couple, really, and I think *Oto-o-san* was lucky to find such a nice woman after our mother died. I should say, rather, that he was fortunate to have a daughter like you to find her for him. He ate his first doughnut in years while he was here. One of Toshiro-san's associates had called on him and had given us a bag of doughnuts, which are becoming quite popular. *Oto-o-san* had not tasted one since the war, when he says you used to help our mother make doughnuts at home (I don't think he liked the store-bought kind). When I think how much Japan has changed in his lifetime I wonder if it could possibly change that much in our lives.

I have thought of going back to Yonago with Hajime to see *Oto-o-san* in August, but it seems as if the whole country is on the move every summer, especially for Memorial Day when everyone goes to pay his respects to the dead, and it is so difficult to get airline or railroad tickets. I would have to stand in line for hours to get tickets for the train a week in advance. So many young people are in college and crowding the trains and planes for their holidays, which doesn't make things any easier for people like me who want to go home for visits. I remember your story about being stuck on a train for fifteen hours without being able to eat anything or go to the toilet.

Hajime returns to school in early April, this time in the first grade. His new school has a swimming pool (you remember how many schools put in pools after the 1964 Olympics here), and Toshiro-san wants him to learn how to swim this year. The East German girls who won the top prizes in swimming at the 1976 Olympics came here afterwards to give our swimming coaches some pointers, and we now have some pretty good Japanese women swimmers. If they are not quite fast enough to beat the East Germans or Americans, at least there are not many who can beat our women.

Hajime will be busy after school now with *juku* (5) or sports. He is only six and not very big, but Toshiro-san wants him to learn *judo*. I'm not so sure. Toshiro-san came with us to the department store to buy Hajime his school clothes and his *randoseru* [school bag carried on the back]. Daimaru [a large Tokyo department store] was terribly crowded so we went to

Mitsukoshi, which was just as crowded. When I discovered that the leather *randoseru* which Hajime wanted cost more than thirty thousand yen [one hundred and fifty dollars], it came as quite a shock, but Toshiro-san said that since we have only one child, and the school bag would last a long time, we might as well get a good one. We also got a notebook and a pencil box. Hajime can't wait to begin school.

They are forecasting a long rainy season and a cold summer this year, so there are predictions that the rice crop will be poor, which will probably be used as an excuse to make food prices even higher. People are even saying that we will have food shortages. It is hard enough to pay for food even now, but I guess that must be true everywhere (6). I was fascinated by what you wrote about America having more acreage planted in grain and soybeans for export to Japan than we have planted ourselves.

Looking out the window, I can see a farmer working in the field behind the house across the street. He grows good vegetables but he is really just waiting for the price of land to go up a little more. Then he will sell it and some builder will put up more apartment blocks. I'm afraid that is what is happening to a lot of good farmland everywhere.

The cherry blossoms are out but only on the *someiyoshino* [an early-blooming variety]. The television news showed huge crowds in Ueno Park even though only about one-tenth of the trees were in bloom. The *bonbori* [traditional lanterns] were hung on the trees, and there were many police to control the crowds—three hundred and thirty thousand people, according to the TV announcer. They were lucky to have such a nice day for the *hanami* [cherry blossom viewing]. Last night we had heavy rains and strong wind, but today is clear and beautiful. I'm rather glad we didn't go to Ueno [a section of Tokyo] though, because not only were there crowds but evidently very noisy crowds. The TV man talked about sixty groups of people having picnics and singing songs under the trees, and he said some young people had brought casette players and were dancing to disco music.

By the way, I bought that feminine hygiene douche that I wrote to you about, and it did make me feel better, if not quite the way Kazuko Fukuda said. My period (Was it you who told me that American women call it "the curse"?) lasted just about as long as ever, but the cramps were not as severe. How much of that is physical and how much psychological I don't know. I heard somewhere that American women have stopped calling it "the curse" and are calling it "my friend" because it means that they are not pregnant. Is that true? We still have our law providing for two days' leave every month for a woman who has menstrual cramps, but the government says that the law is really just for women with certain kinds of jobs, such as assembly line work where an employee cannot stop, or a job that keeps a woman on her feet all day or obliges her to perform heavy labor. A few years ago, Keio Hospital in Tokyo started cutting the pay of female employees when they took days off for menstrual cramps, and some women who lived in dormitories were ordered back to work. Some older women were ordered to report their vaginal temperatures regularly so that it could be determined if they were still ovulating. In another case, a woman of forty-seven was asked to speak to the head of the company about why she was taking two days off every month for menstrual cramps. Do American women get time off with pay every month by law? Do they take advantage of the law the way some Japanese women do? The feminists here oppose the law. They say that laws like this confirm the average man's conception of women as being generally inferior and handicap us in the struggle for equality. Anyway, I like the douche and I think Toshiro-san likes it, too. He and I have agreed not to have any more children, incidentally (7). We love Hajime, and perhaps it would be nice for him to have a sister or brother (They tell me it's easier to have two children than one because they can entertain each other), but it's too difficult today to find housing for a large family like our family in Yonago. The world nowadays is just too crowded. I have read about the people in America who oppose abortion. They are not very realistic, I think. If they saw the congestion in countries like Japan, I'm sure many of them would change their minds (8).

Sachiko

13 April

Dear Chie,

Your letter arrived right after I wrote to you yesterday. Too bad you were not able to get to Trinidad for the Carnival as you had planned. Maybe next year. Did you know that Mitsubishi and some other Japanese companies were helping to build a government steel plant on the island? Toshiro-san says he heard that his company had looked at possible sites in the area but had decided that there were better opportunities elsewhere.

Although Hajime was a little timid at first, he now seems happy in his new school. Whether he is smart enough to get into Todai University (9) remains to be seen. Toshiro-san is very hopeful. I remember the discussion you and he had about education when you were here and how disturbed you were about the pressure that children are under these days to do well in school so that they can be successful in later life. It is true that hundreds of our teenagers commit suicide every year (10). A boy in the neighborhood took his life in February. Toshiro-san says you should remember that not all of those suicides are related to poor marks or entrance exams, although that is the biggest reason among senior high school students. We don't like the pressure to which children are subjected, either, but we haven't much choice. When Toshiro-san came back from a business trip to Australia last year, he talked about the great open spaces there and the lack of pressure. He said it would be wonderful for Hajime if he could grow up in that kind of country. Then he came down to earth and realized the difficulties.

In any event, Hajime seems quite bright, and we are lucky to live in a place where the local school has such a fine reputation. He is off to a good start, at least. The expenses of having a child of Hajime's age are not too great. Even so, we are keeping our fingers crossed about Toshiro-san's summer bonus. At this point it seems there should be no problem about that, but we remember a few years ago when the sudden jump in oil prices hurt business and many companies, including Toshiro-san's, had to reduce, or even omit, the yearend bonus.

Tamiko-san is happy that March is behind us. It has been the busiest time of year for her. You remember the graduation parties, the parties to show appreciation for teachers, and so forth. The new term has now begun. Tamiko-san's older boy, Ken, is starting senior high school, so he has gone through what they call *shiken jigoku* [examination hell]. He was on the gymnastics team and was scheduled to participate in the prefecture contest, which his team won last year. This year he felt sure that he would win but did not go because he had to study for the exams. It was a hard decision for a boy of that age to make, and we all felt proud about the way he handled it. Tamiko-san was very nervous, as I guess we all were, and we had a big celebration when Ken did well on the examinations. Tamiko-san's younger son, Tadashi, is interested in chemistry and wants to go to the United States to study. He just started junior high and is already reading college level chemistry texts.

Sachiko

May 6

Dear Chie,

With the warm weather here to stay, I find myself thinking of that big Central Park you have in New York—I would love to see it with all the daffodils in bloom as you describe it—and wishing we had more parks here. One reason we chose to live so far outside Tokyo was the sight of green fields, but as I think I wrote you, the fields are disappearing as more houses go up.

Hibiya Public Park in the city is not very big, and the grounds of the Imperial Palace, as you know, are open to the public only two days a year—New Year's Day and the emperor's birthday. His birthday was a week ago yesterday, and since it was a Sunday there were enormous crowds. The last big parcel of good land in Tokyo is the old Tachikawa Air

Base, which is twenty-seven times the size of Hibiya Public Park, and one of the newspapers is campaigning to have it turned into Tachikawa Forest. The local community group gave a slide show last evening and we saw pictures of your Central Park. Do you really live only one block away? And is it really three hundred and forty hectares [eight hundred and forty acres]? That is eight times the size of Komazawa Park in Tokyo. We also saw Forest Park in St. Louis, Belle Isle in Detroit, Grant Park in Chicago, Golden Gate Park in San Francisco, the Bois de Boulogne in Paris, the Alameda in Madrid, Prater Park in Vienna, and Regent's Park, Hyde Park, and some other parks in London.

You might think everyone would want to see more parks in Tokyo, and that there would be very little opposition. The truth is, many people would rather see the Tachikawa land used for housing. It's so convenient to the center of Tokyo, and four hundred and eighty hectares [one thousand and eighty-five acres] would provide space for many, many apartment houses. Hibiya Public Park is only sixteen hectares [less than forty acres] to give you an idea of the size. Shizen Kyoikuen [Nature Education Park] in Minato Ward, where the big chinquapin trees grow, is twenty hectares, and there are thirty-five thousand square meters of land adjoining that park where the Shirogane Guest House used to be. A company bought the land to put up a hotel; some people, including me, think it should be saved for green space. I'm sure there are some greedy real estate and construction interests that are leading the fight against turning the Tachikawa property and smaller parcels of land into parkland. I think the people who listen to them are being very shortsighted. The population of Tokyo has been increasing so fast. They say that if the growth continues at the present rate the city will have nearly thirty-five million people by the end of the century. I cannot comprehend such a large number, and it is frightening to think about having so many people without some tranquil green places for peaceful contemplation.

There was a local politician at the community meeting last evening, and she said Japan has a long history of destroying urban greenery. She talked about a book published in 1894, the same year as the famous Yakumo Koizumi [Lafcadio Hearn] book. This book said the Japanese were concerned only about small immediate profits and that the whole country was destroying nature. That would seem to be an area in which women could play an active role. What do you think? If you could see how much beautiful landscape is being bulldozed to make room for more housing, I think you would feel as strongly as I that something must be done before it is too late.

We have a tradition of working together in this country and solving problems by mutual effort. I'm told that it goes back to the time when this was a rural nation of rice-growers. A single family working alone could not produce rice very efficiently, since it took at least twenty people to build and maintain the irrigation system, so a dozen families would pool their efforts and produce so much rice there was some left over to sell. I guess that's still true, and we still co-operate in other ways. Certainly we have been successful in reducing the overall rate of population growth. Now if only we could cooperate in protecting the environment. If we don't, what kind of Japan will Hajime and his cousins grow up in? I wonder how the Americans and Europeans were able to create all those parks. If they could do it, we certainly should be able to, and I think women would support efforts to create more parkland if only we had effective leadership. You say that your apartment is not very big, but I imagine it is enormous compared to the size of most Japanese apartments, and even Japanese houses. With so many of us living in such cramped quarters, we need as much open space out-of-doors as possible. It's frustrating to feel that relatively few people really care about things that to me are just about the most precious things in life.

Sachiko

15

20 *May*

Dear Chie,

Today the weather is quite warm and Toshiro-san has taken Hajime to watch some men fly kites. I'm feeling lazy, but I did want to write to you.

Do you remember my telling you about Kazuko Fukuda, the woman down the hall who spends her time in the *pachinko* parlor? There is something peculiar about her, although I can't put my finger on what it is. She lives very simply and avoids people. Some of my neighbors were quite surprised that she went into town with me. It is almost as if she were trying to hide something, or at least that is what the neighbors say. I must say she seems nice enough to me, and they may just be overly suspicious. She is older than most of us and lives alone, and I don't know whether she is a widow, a divorcee, or just a woman who never married. I think she must have been quite attractive when she was younger. Anyway, she called on me yesterday and wanted to know if I would like to buy some life insurance, which I politely declined. Quite a few women seem to be involved in that sort of work.

Again, it made me think how much Japan has changed — especially for women. You told me you had taken photographs of some women's liberation movement activities in America, and I read some things written by that French woman Simone de Beauvoir that had been translated into Japanese. I don't think she has any idea how far we Japanese women have come since the time when we had no rights at all, only duties. At our P.T.A. meeting the other day there was a speaker who cited some Japanese proverbs to show the menial position that women had in traditional Japanese society. I remember one was *Shichinin no ko wo nasu tomo onna ni* kokoro o yurusuna ["Never trust a woman, even though she has borne you seven children"]. Toshiro-san says that his father can remember when it was common for a Japanese man to write to a friend and refer to his *gusai* [stupid wife] and his *tonji* [pig son], and Toshiro-san's father is not that old.

The P.T.A. speaker told us that a man used to be able to divorce his wife simply by giving her a *mikudari-han* [literally, three and a half lines], a letter only three and a half lines long notifying her of his intent, and that even as recently as the early part of this century a man could divorce his wife simply by going to the ward office, or town office, and obliterating her name from the family register. Any of seven reasons was acceptable, and they included talkativeness, a communicable disease (Wasn't it you who told me that tuberculosis used to be very common in Japan?), jealousy, and refusal to serve her husband's parents. If a woman could not produce a child, it was always assumed to be her fault, not the husband's, and that, too, was grounds for divorce. I remember your telling me once about seeing the neighbor's daughter-in-law crying outside the door back in Yonago because her husband had been ordered by his mother to get a divorce. You said the mother was never satisfied, and that the son was married three times. According to the P.T.A. speaker, a wife could be punished for adultery under the old law but an adulterous husband was punished only if the other woman's husband took the matter to court.

You write about the feminist movement in the United States. I think it is regaining strength here. There was a time, you know, when the word *feminisuto* [feminist] was used to mean a man who was nice to women. A lot of Japanese feminist groups sprang up before 1975, which was International Women's Year. The one that attracted the most attention, unfortunately, was the Chupiren group, which wore pink helmets and got a lot of headlines. They stormed the homes of divorced male celebrities, demanding that they pay more alimony to their ex-wives. They raided the offices of well-known men who were openly unfaithful to their wives. What finally set them back was the defeat of Misako Enoki, the leader of the Women's Party, who tried to win election in June 1977 to the *Sangiin* [upper house of the Diet]. The Chupiren group backed her, and she announced that if she was not elected she would abandon the movement and devote herself to being a good wife and mother. When she lost, she carried out her threat and the media said that the women's movement in Japan was dead. The term *uman ribu* [women's lib] that came from America is dead, and nobody is sorry. The Chupiren group made it seem like hysterical radicalism which did not help anybody. Women here are still called *kanjo no dobutsu* [animals of emotion], but feminism is gaining strength.

I think most Japanese women today would prefer not to marry oldest sons whose mothers are still alive, and that very few wish to live with their husbands' parents. Toshiro-san is the oldest son, as you know, but his parents are very pleasant and I am happy to serve them when they come to visit. If I did not like them I don't think it would be necessary for me to go out of my way for them. It's not like the old days, at least not in this case. I think you said James-san had no parents, but what if he did? What would your obligations be? Your comments on his sisters were very funny. Do they know how you feel? Does James-san know? How does he feel about having a hippie sister who lives in a wigwam in Arizona?

As you can see, I am getting quite interested in the differences between American society and ours, especially in regard to women. I always look forward to reading your letters about life in the United States. It must be strange for you to live in a country whose ways are so different from ours.

Sachiko

24 *June*

Dear Chie,

Please forgive me for not writing in more than a month. I have not really been all that busy, just a little depressed. Perhaps what got me down was what Toshiro-san told me last week about a woman in his office. No, it wasn't anything like that, but what he said about this woman made me think that perhaps I should not have married so young.

Oh, please don't think I am unhappy with Toshiro-san or Hajime. Nothing could be more untrue. Still, a young woman in Japan today has such freedom. The woman in Toshiro-san's office is just a clerk yet she is going to Hawaii for her holiday. I asked how much money she made, and it turned out that her base pay comes to about 116,200 yen a month [about four hundred and eight-five dollars] and her midsummer bonus is going to be at least a month's pay and maybe two months'. The package trip to Honolulu on Japan Air Lines is going to cost one hundred and sixty-five thousand yen [just under seven hundred dollars at the time] which includes six nights at a hotel in Waikiki. She's twenty-four and she still lives at home, so she has little to spend her money on except herself.

The young women I see in Tokyo these days are in many cases like that clerk, I guess, and you should see the clothes they wear. Of course, if I had stayed home in Yonago it would not have been easy for me to find a job that paid well, and when Toshiro-san and I were married he wanted me to stop working, so perhaps I am just fantasizing. Still, I have so much energy, I have extra time, I'm not stupid, and I really should be able to figure out a way to bring in some money. We could certainly use it, and even if we didn't need the money, I think a woman should have a life of her own and not just live for her husband and children. If that sounds like I read the book you told me about, the one by Betty Friedan, it's because I did. I think she is right.

I know that our mother really ran the family in Yonago, and I know that having control of the finances puts me in an important position in my own family. It's just that there really aren't enough finances to control. I confess that I envy my big sister in New York with her career. It may not make you rich, as you say, but it does give you a certain amount of independence.

Sachiko

2 September

Dear Chie,

Time goes by so quickly. Our only summer holiday consisted of taking Hajime to the mineral springs at Atagawa for three days. He loved it, and I will never forget the absolute bliss of the cool evening Toshiro-san and I spent together in the *rotenburo* [hot outdoor bath] with Mt. Amagi rising above us in the moonlight while dozens of squid-fishing boats, each with a lantern hung from its prow, danced about on the Pacific below.

If only we could afford a villa in a place like that. I don't suppose we ever shall, but it is something to dream about, isn't it? We do try to save. I guess all Japanese do. I read somewhere that the average Japanese has savings of over ten thousand dollars, more than twice what the average American has (11).

When you were in high school, did you think our parents were proud of you? I know that's a silly question, but I wondered. I read lately that American high school students and Japanese high school students were asked that question, and eighty-six percent of the American students said yes, less than five percent said no. Among the Japanese students, only about forty-six percent said yes; more than fifty percent said no. I'm not sure what that means, and I can't remember how I felt about it.

Do you suppose the feeling of not being admired by their parents has something to do with the high rate of suicide among Japanese high school students? I know I wrote about that in my last letter, and please don't think I am dwelling on morbid subjects. I am just curious. Do you rememember my friend Fumiko Kobayashi? She loaned me a book by a university professor named Taki Sugiyama Lebra, *Japanese Patterns of Behavior*, and she writes that death, particularly voluntary death, is surrounded in this country by a heroic, romantic, aesthetic, and moral aura. She says we often find it hard to communicate and use suicide as a way to make our ideas, or beliefs, or sufferings known. I don't know whether I believe that or not.

There must be a better way to express feelings, don't you think? Life is much too interesting to throw away.

Sachiko

7 October

Dear Chie,

How kind you were to send me the sweaters. Toshiro-san wore his to the company outing — no wives invited, of course — and Hajime will hardly let me take his sweater off even when it is time for his bath.

Toshiro-san, by the way, will be away for the next two weeks on a business trip. You know what we always say: a good husband is one who enjoys good health and is not at home. In some ways, it will be relaxing to have him away. Still, with Hajime at school almost all day now the apartment seems empty and I will miss Toshiro-san. Not that I see very much of him even when he is *not* away on business. He has to get up early for his hour-and-a-half trip to the office each morning and he often works late, so I do have some lonely times, even with Yoko-san and Tamiko-san living nearby. Did I tell you that Tamiko-san was captain of her P.T.A. volleyball team? Her sons are very athletic, too, and since her husband is not at all athletic she says it must come from the Nishio side of the family.

Quite a few women in this area now commute to offices in the city every morning just like the men, though of course they are women who have no children or whose children are grown. I can only work part time, and there are very few decent part-time jobs. To help make some extra money, I have started typing again. You saw the big old Japanese typewriter I have, the one we bought second-hand a few years ago. I remember how carefully James-san studied it and how he found it so hard to understand how we Japanese could be so successful in business without efficient electric typewriters and word processors using the twenty-six-letter *romaji* [roman] alphabet. Given our three different alphabets (12) and the hundreds of characters we use, I don't see how we could ever develop machines like that for writing. This machine of mine is primitive by comparison, I guess, and it is slower than writing the characters by hand. Still, the word is getting about that I can turn out typewritten business letters, contracts, and manuscripts for publishers, so I'm getting quite a number of customers, who pay pretty well, often when I least expect it. It is not the most dependable source of income, I know. Still, it helps.

Toshiro-san thinks he has a good future with his company. You may remember that he used to be the number two man in his labor union, and higher-ups in the labor union generally become higher-ups in the company management. The present, he says, is just something we will have to go through. He works long hours and it is hard to put much aside from his pay. If we do not save, how will we ever be able to afford a house, or a car, or college tuition for Hajime? Toshiro-san has been reluctant to have me work, but he knows what I'm doing. If only I could find something more lucrative. Of course I am the one who handles the family funds. I was surprised to read in your letter that the woman in the family does not generally do that in America. Does James-san give you an allowance? I don't think I should like that. I give Toshiro-san an allowance, and he is pretty good about not asking for more.

Forgive my bad writing, Chie-san. I wish I could express myself the way you can. Fortunately, James-san cannot read Japanese and will not know how poorly I write. Also, I write things to you that I would not want anyone else in the world to see.

Sachiko

Dear Chie,

Last Sunday was election day and it rained so hard that the government had to go on radio and television urging people to come out and vote. Typhoon Eighteen was the second worst since the Pacific War, and those of us who did vote got absolutely drenched. The voter turnout was scarcely sixty-eight percent, which is very low. That is partly because young people are not too interested in politics but mostly because of the foul weather.

We still have more women voters than men voters, yet not too many women get elected to the Diet and most of those that do are elected to the *Sangiin* [upper house] which has less power than the *Shugiin* [lower house]. Many are former schoolteachers. The *Sangiin* has two hundred and fifty-two members of whom one hundred are elected not from the prefectures but by nationwide balloting, so the chief qualification of many is simply that they have national recognition. The old movie star Yoshiko Yamaguchi — now Yoshiko Otaka — for example, and the television actress Akiko Santo. Also Aiko Anzai, who is now Aiko Shimura. When she sang on the radio they used to call her *"Uta-no-obasan"* [Singing Aunt]. Yoko-san and I were talking about all this and we agreed that with women voters outnumbering men voters it is strange that we do not elect more women to the Diet — we elected thirty-four when we first got the vote in 1946 — and that the ones who stand for election are not better qualified. What kind of women do the Americans elect to Congress, I wonder?

Unlike you, Yoko-san is not much of a letter writer, so you probably have not heard that she has a job. Her two little girls are now in school all day, so she had a lot of extra time and decided to put her training in chemistry to work. It's a small company, but as a subsidiary of a much larger one it seems to be well situated and the pay is evidently good, at least for a woman, not to mention all the fringe benefits such as life insurance and vacations. Best of all, the office is not in downtown Tokyo so it takes her less than half an hour to get to work.

As for me, I continue to live from day to day with no great plans for the future. I know I should make more money so that I can do some of the things I want to do (such as coming to visit you), and save for Hajime's education, but it's hard to know how to do it.

The leaves that survived the typhoons are beginning to turn, and Fuji looks awesome in the clear air. I hope you can return before long to visit us again and enjoy the changing seasons as we do, although I suppose you must have pleasant days in New York, too. Someday I hope to see all of the things you have written about, although I don't think I should like some of it, such as the graffiti in the subways and the women who live in the streets. We do have some trouble with drunks in Shinjuku [a Tokyo district noted for its department stores and its nightlife], but generally people here are as orderly as always and the streets, the subways and subway platforms are kept neat and clean. Yes, and our banknotes are still new and crisp, not like the American currency you wrote about. Is it really so dirty and torn and so often taped together? Don't the banks there destroy old currency and issue new notes? I'm surprised that people don't object.

Yesterday, I took Hajime into Tokyo and went to Daimaru to buy him a new jacket for winter. Prices for everything are higher than last year, but at the station I saw a florist selling white chrysanthemums for only three hundred yen [a dollar fifty]. That was for a big bunch, and I don't think she gave me a special price or anything. They really look lovely over the stereo. You asked about the pay phones and it still costs only ten yen [less than a nickel] for three minutes. Is it really as expensive as you say in parts of the United States? The inflation here is worse this year because of higher oil prices, they say, but the recession seems to be over. You wrote that New York City was almost bankrupt a few years ago, and Tokyo was having trouble, too. Things are better now.

Fortunately, we did not have to lay off police officers the way New York did. I worry about your safety in that city. You say that it is really quite safe where you live, but the figures I read about the crime there are frightening. As you know, we still have the lowest crime rate in the world, even though we have a lot fewer police per citizen than you do (13). They say it's partly because of our laws against firearms and narcotics, although many people maintain that it is simply a matter of our all growing up with certain shared moral standards maintained by families and schools. I think you have more murders and robberies in one day in New York City than we have in a whole year in all of Japan. That may be an exaggeration, but I read something of the sort. Please be careful.

Sachiko

Dear Chie,

More leaves are turning color now and I find myself thinking about how cold the old house at Yonago gets in winter, especially the toilet (14). Do you remember? My friend Fumiko-san's father collapsed from cerebral apoplexy last winter, and the doctor said it was because the toilet room was so cold. Going from a warm place into the cold room caused certain blood vessels to contract sharply, which made his blood pressure take a sudden jump. The doctor said it was not uncommon among older people going to the toilet in the winter, and I'm worried about Father in that cold house.

I telephoned to Mariko-san in Yonago about it (she sends her greetings, by the way), and she agreed that we ought to do something about the situation. If we sisters each contributed five thousand yen [about twenty-five dollars], we could have the old privy converted into a Western-style, sit-down commode, which would be more comfortable for *Oto-o-san* [Father] than having to squat, and an electric space heater. The commode would have pipe rails bolted to the sides, and it would have a lever to raise or lower the seat, depending on whether one wanted to sit or crouch. Also, there would be an electric heating unit to warm the seat so that Father would not be exposed to a sudden shock of cold.

What do you think, Chie-san? I'm sure Tamiko-san and Yoko-san will chip in, and it really should be a gift from all of us. *Oto-o-san* is old-fashioned, I know, but I'm sure he would be pleased and not offended. It would make a nice New Year's gift. We are all so accustomed to flush toilets that we tend to forget that we grew up without such things and that *Oto-o-san* still lives in the traditional way (plus television, of course — he does spend a lot of time watching television).

Sachiko

16 *December*

Dear Chie,

Here it is almost the end of another year and I am writing partly to wish you a happy new year. This one has gone by all too quickly.

It was not a good year for our *nakaudo* (15). He died (I think it was lung cancer) and then she had a stroke, leaving her with limited use of her right arm and leg. Her son suggested that she come to live with him and his wife, but she worries that she might not get along well with her daughter-in-law and might not be able to invite her friends over to visit.

The stores are all decorated for Christmas as usual, which must be strange for older people who remember the days before the war when Christmas was only for foreigners. It's rather amazing, I think, that a country like this where less than one percent of the people are practicing Christians should make such a fuss about Christmas, but we do have a way of adopting foreign customs, don't we, and the idea of gift-giving is pretty deeply ingrained in us. Of course I have grown up seeing Christmas trees and Santa Claus pictures, but I understand that giving *oseibo* (16) was common even before the Americans introduced Christmas after the war. Every big department store now has a woman dressed in a Santa Claus costume — she's called "Sister Santa" at Matsuzakaya — and I understand that people come in with their children, find out what the children want, and then have the store wrap up the toys or whatever in Christmas paper with a note from Santa enclosed. Hajime doesn't believe in Santa Claus anymore but he's still very excited about Christmas. The emphasis on children is the big difference between Christmas-giving and our old custom of giving *oseibo*, and stores are pushing Christmas harder every year. I bought a

28

gift set of skin cream for Hajime's teacher as an *oseibo*. She's really a very nice woman, and I do want her to think well of us, but I must say some parents are rather excessive in their gifts to teachers. I found some papercraft that I think you will like. I will airmail them to you.

I also bought the new best selling novel that everybody is reading, and I was going to write to you about it, but when I thought about what I had read I realized that it was really trash. I cannot imagine what all the excitement is about or why the young man who wrote it won a prize. I was expecting something more. Maybe it's just me, but if this is literature then the standards have certainly changed.

James-san may be right in his theory about why Japanese best sellers have sales so much larger than those of most American best sellers (17). We do read a lot of books just to kill time, as I guess people must do everywhere. There are some other factors that he should consider, though. Japanese publishers don't put out nearly so many new titles each year as American publishers, for example (18), and the titles they do publish get heavily promoted. Also, I understand that quite a few million Americans cannot read or write in any language, whereas we have practically no illiteracy. Maybe that is because our students spend more time in school than Americans do (19). You might tell James-san that another reason why we buy so many books is that we don't have many lending libraries the way you do in America.

Toshiro-san got his yearend bonus, for which we are thankful. Four months' pay is what we were counting on and we were not disappointed (20). We both hope the new year will be a good one for you and James-san.

Sachiko

Dear Chie,

None of us got home to Yonago for New Year's, but we did speak with *Oto-o-san* on the telephone and he is delighted with our gift. Thank you so much for helping. He reminded me of the New Year celebrations we used to have back in Yonago, although I am really too young to remember very clearly helping to make *mochi* (21). Now, of course, we buy *mochi* ready-made in the shops along with *osechi-ryori* [special New Year's food]; it may have been fun to make *mochi* at home, as you say, but I don't know of anyone who still does it anymore.

You wrote last year about the fancy New Year's Eve party that you and James-san attended in New York. I wish I could have seen you. Here, of course, we celebrate privately, although Toshiro-san got home very late one night two weeks ago after his *bonenkai* [forget-the-old-year party] with his office colleagues, and he did not feel too well the next day. He said that he had gone on to a *nijikai* [second party] and that some of the men had gone to a *sanjikai* [third party]. What most people do now on New Year's Eve is watch the *kohaku utagassen* [white and red singing competition] on television. NHK [the government television company] has promoted it into a sort of tradition, which is all right if you like pop music, I suppose.

Last year, as I wrote to you, we visited the Meiji Shrine (22) at New Year's. It was not nearly so pretty as it is in early December when the colorful foliage is still on the trees, and it was so crowded that we decided this year to visit Yoko-san on New Year's Day. Toshiro-san's junior called on us the next day. Nothing remarkable about the visits, just business talk — and endless cigarettes. The new year has started out well for us, even without our having made any contribution or having said prayers at a Shinto shrine. Toshiro-san feels sure he is going to get his promotion, and although it will not mean a big increase in income it is encouraging. He will have more responsibility but he's afraid that he will also have to do more business entertaining. Fortunately, he is not like most husbands, who stop off somewhere on the way home (23). Are American husbands like that? What about James-san? Toshiro-san does get home late quite often, but he always lets me know in advance or calls to tell me and he has hardly ever had too much to drink the way so many men do (24).

Toshiro-san is very loyal to his company, of course (25). Most Japanese employees are, and I understand that. It probably explains why our companies have done so well, but it also has a lot to do with making women here unhappy (26). Younger women today, I gather, are putting pressure on their husbands not to work late, so the men who stay late at the office tend to be older men who are worried about being promoted and want to appear especially hard-working.

The only pressure I have put on Toshiro-san is to give up smoking, and he has not had a cigarette in the new year, I am happy to say. He says he made a New Year's resolution. Whatever it is, I am glad, and I have had all his clothes cleaned to get the tobacco smell out of them. He still comes home with his hair and clothes smelling of cigarette smoke because most of the other men in his office smoke (27). I was surprised to hear from you that so many women smoke in America. Here it is still relatively rare to see a woman smoke. You write that one American cigarette company has used women's liberation as a theme to boost its sales, which I find really shocking. I mean, if more American women now smoke than American men, what does smoking have to do with "liberation"? James-san is the only American I have ever got to know. I don't know any American women. The ones in the movies are quite different from Japanese women, but I never realized how strange American women were until you remarked about how much they smoke. The tobacco people are obviously exploiting women when they use that "liberation" idea. Haven't women been exploited long enough?

Somebody (Was it you?) told me that more Americans die every year from causes related to cigarette smoking than died from the atomic bomb attacks on Hiroshima and Nagasaki put together. I think a lot of people here are beginning to realize how dangerous smoking is and are giving it up, although you wouldn't know it to see all the men smoking on the trains, on the streets, in restaurants, even on subway platforms except during the rush hours, when it is forbidden. It's interesting to hear from you that smoking is becoming socially unacceptable in many circles over there; it's hard to believe that this could happen in Japan, but let's hope so. I certainly pray that Hajime is strong enough not to be pressured into smoking. Tobacco is still a government monopoly here and I should think the government would be more responsible, knowing what is now known about how many people are killed by smoking. They should do more to discourage the practice if only to reduce the widows' benefits that taxpayers must bear.

Anyway, I have many things to make me happy as we start the new year, and I hope you have, too. Whether one is happy or not is hard to say without a basis for comparison, of course. I think I am happy, yet I know there are many things I would like to do, such as visiting you and James-san. That seems completely out of reach at this point, I'm afraid, so I must content myself with hoping that it can be managed somehow in the future. Perhaps the fact that it must be postponed will make it an even greater pleasure when it finally happens.

Sachiko

Dear Chie,

Today was *Hina Matsuri* [Girls' Day Festival] so this evening I went to see Yoko-san and her daughters. Michiko is seven now and Mariko nearly six. They were delighted to show off their dolls and the miniature furniture, dinner services, musical instruments, and so forth. Hajime came with me and was thoroughly bored, I think, although he was polite and he did enjoy the rice cooked with red beans, the diamond-shaped cakes, and the fruit-shaped candies.

I remember growing up with some of those dolls, especially the *dairi-sama* [dolls representing the emperor and empress] that belonged to mother's mother. They still sit there on the top shelf of the *hina-dan* [doll stand] just as they did when I was a little girl. Do you remember? Now Michiko and Mariko have the lower shelves pretty well filled with *sannin-kanjo* [three ladies-in-waiting], *gonin-bayashi* [five musicians], pages, and guards. It's a nice tradition, I guess, but I hate to think of all the money that is spent on those dolls. You told me once that yours were traded for food during the war. How sad that must have been for you.

The dolls, you may recall, have their faces quite heavily made up, and I read recently that there is a painting more than a thousand years old at the Imperial Museum at Nara (28) showing the goddess of beauty with her lips painted bright crimson. I haven't been to Nara since our junior high school class made the trip. Did yours go, too? I don't recall much about it except the excitement of being away from home. Anyway, the tradition of using cosmetics is very old in this country. I have some memory of Mother buying skin cream but I don't know what brand it was. Do you have any idea?

I do clearly recall Mother using a mixture of sake and glycerin to make a hand lotion that kept her hands from being rough and red; she said that women in the country used it to disguise the fact that they had to work in the rice fields and that she had learned it from her grandmother. The old folk cosmetics still have a certain market. There is a little shop in Asakusa [subsquent inquiries revealed the address: Hyaku-suke Shoten, 2-14-2 Asakusa, Daito-ku, Tokyo] specializing in stage makeup that sells *beni*, a lip rouge made from the petals of a *beni-hana* [literally, red flower] that are crushed to obtain the color. They say that the best *beni* used to be made at two o'clock in the morning on the coldest days of winter. I don't know how true that is. I do know that some women with allergies still use *beni* instead of modern lipsticks. They apply it only to the middle of the lower lip, and when it's applied heavily it takes on a greenish gold tint. A friend of mine showed me a jar of it once — it comes in a little ceramic bowl — and you could see the shadings of green and gold when it caught the light. Sometimes it's mixed with honey, which adds a shine and makes it sweet-tasting. They say it prevents lip chapping, but that is true with any lipstick, I think.

Some people still use products that go back to the days before we had soap. I guess it was hard to make soap without animal fats or coconut oil. Anyway, the pre-soap products are still with us. For shampoos, there is *kami no arai ko* [hair wash powder], which looks like clay and used to come in packages but now comes in plastic envelopes. You mix the powder with hot water to form a paste and rub it into your scalp. In the old days it took seven changes of water to rinse it out, and the water had to be heated on a charcoal stove for each change. Women in the country would wash their hair at the river's edge and rinse it in the stream, although that could only have been done in warm weather. Can you picture those women lying on the riverbank with their long black hair streaming off into the current? Thank heaven for hot running water.

Didn't you tell me once that our mother washed her hair with *funori* [a yellow-colored seaweed]. I read about that. They use it to make a kind of liquid starch for fine kimono. It is also used unstrained and mixed with *udonko* [a flour used in making *udon*, the thick Japanese noodles so popular at lunch] to produce a shampoo. I haven't used either *kami no arai ko* or *funori*, but I gather that they are quite satisfactory, leaving the hair feeling clean and with more body so that it is easy to work with.

Between washings, women used to use oil from camellia flowers on their hair, and some women still wash their hair only a few times a year, using camellia oil for everyday hair grooming. They rub the oil into their hair and scalp and then comb their hair over and over with wooden combs that have cotton or artificial hair between the teeth to remove excess oil.

As you may or may not have heard, we've had quite a scandal in connection with modern cosmetics. You probably haven't heard, unless someone wrote to you about it, because even though it has been going on for several years such things don't generally get into foreign newspapers. I can't tell you all the juicy details now, but I'll try to write again soon.

The weather is turning warm again and Toshiro-san finally stopped wearing the long underwear he has put on every day since December. I almost wish we had an air conditioner. Do you have one in New York? Toshiro-san is against it. He is very modern in some ways, and in other ways very traditional. Tamiko-san and her husband sleep on Western-style beds, Toshiro-san says he prefers the *futon* (29). Not that we have room for Western-style beds, but he says he would rather sleep the traditional way even if we did have room. He also prefers eating at home with *hashi* (30), even though we have silverware which I like to use for certain dishes. Tamiko-san's husband is dead-set against her working, even though they could use the money. Toshiro-san is not enthusiastic about the idea of my working, but he does let me do my typing since I do it at home and I think he could be persuaded to let me do more.

Sachiko

30 *March*

Dear Chie,

I promised to tell you about the big cosmetic industry scandal we had here. It involved something called *kokuhisho* [black skin syndrome], and it evidently came from using any of a number of different popular brands of skin creams and sun lotions. Quite a few women had the trouble, which began with irritation and progressed to skin discoloration (31). There was an article in *Shukanshincho* [a weekly magazine] about Yuko Uboshita. She is an Osaka woman who bought some sun lotion in the summer of 1973. It irritated her face, her cheeks became very red, and when she went back to the store where she had bought it she was given a skin cream. She used that, and where her cheeks had been red they began to take on a stained appearance. She tried to use a foundation to cover up the stain, and where she had used the foundation the area of discoloration expanded. By November 1976, her cheeks were a dark brown and she complained to the manufacturer. Someone from the cosmetic company brought over some massage cream and a therapeutic ointment. She used these, but her skin kept getting darker and darker. Her husband said it was probably not a good idea to use the massage cream and ointment. She replied that *he* had told her to use what the manufacturer brought over. They got into a big fight, and by January 1977 her skin looked so bad that her husband left her. I guess her disposition had also got worse; I know mine would have. They actually got a legal separation, and she thought many times of committing suicide; after all, she felt so ugly that she could not leave her house. The more things she tried, the worse her skin became. Finally, she stopped using anything, and her skin condition improved to the point where she got in touch with other women who had had bad reactions to various cosmetics and they organized a No-Makeup Club.

Some women still sometimes use *nuka* [the outer part of the grain that is removed in polishing rice] for their skin. They occasionally mix it with *aburakasu* [the hulls from camellia seeds] and *karasu-uri* [an autumn plant with bright red pods]. These are put into a cotton bag about ten centimeters [roughly four inches] square which is then wet and rubbed briskly over the body. And women still make a thick syrup by mixing *kurozato* [black sugar, although it is actually dark brown] with hot water and rubbing it on their faces and bodies. They wait a few minutes and rinse it off. They may also use a dried *hechima* [a kind of gourd] as a bath sponge (It's supposed to be a good skin toner), or a body lotion made by cutting the *hechima* stem into small pieces, putting them in a jar, and waiting a few days. Have you ever heard of these things? I wonder if our mother ever used them? Do you remember?

One of the more exotic old beauty products still available is *uguisu no fun* [nightingale droppings]. It used to be sold in bird stores and still is sold in a small bird store in Shimbashi [Kakimi, 1-7 14 Nisi Shimbashi, Minato-ku, Tokyo]. It's measured out and sold in beautiful little square boxes (they were evidently the traditional measures). You're supposed to grind the droppings in a *suribachi* [a rough-sided bowl] with a wooden pestle before you apply them to your face. You add a tiny spoonful to a small basin of hot water, cup your hands, and then bathe your face and neck, or you add it to *nuka* and rub it on your body. The *uguisu no fun* sold today comes from a government-inspected nightingale farm in Gifu Prefecture. There was apparently a problem of impurities in the product some time ago, but it is now quite safe. They process it, and grind it, and sell it for one thousand yen [about five dollars] in packets with a cherry blossom design.

They say that in the old days of Japan the back of a woman's neck was considered the most sexy part of her body. Women then used to whiten their faces and the backs of their necks with *neri oshiroi*. It was made of clay and some kind of earth and came in liquid, powder, or cake form. It also contained lead carbonate and cadmia. Many court ladies died of lead poisoning or cadmium poisoning, and so did quite a few courtesans and actors who wore heavy makeup. You may remember the *Itai Itai* [literally ouch! ouch!] disease we had in connection with cadmium pollution in the 1960s when I was in high school (32). Cadmium poisoning is evidently very painful. They used to show films in school of women dying agonizing deaths from the effects of using *oshiroi* to warn girls against cosmetics that contained lead or cadmium.

Tamiko-san has a friend who had trouble with *her* skin. She'd been using skin cream — I forget which brand — and her face got so bad that she stopped going to P.T.A. meetings. Tamiko-san says the woman looked just awful. There have been stories in the newspapers about women who gave up jobs or were refused employment because of their skin, and some found themselves ostracized by their husbands' families. That was true of Tamiko-san's friend. Tamiko-san learned from another friend about a new line of cosmetics that are sold door-to-door and at home parties. I don't know how it is in America, but most cosmetic manufacturers here never explain what ingredients they use, so if you have an allergy there is no way of knowing whether an item contains something that might give you a bad reaction. These new cosmetics — the brand name is Noevir (33) — use only herbal ingredients so they're much safer, Tamiko-san says, and she thinks I might do well selling them. I don't know. I've never considered doing anything like that. Still, I must say I'm interested, and I've begun making inquiries about it. Selling cosmetics might not be a bad idea, especially if the products are as good as Tamiko-san's friend says they are. I'll write again when I know more.

Sachiko

18 *May*

Dear Chie,

I just returned from the wedding of my young friend Kaori Ochiai, and I was thinking about you on my way home. Imagine my surprise and pleasure upon my return at finding your letter in the afternoon mail (34).

Perhaps I have not mentioned Kaori-san before. She and her new husband met at the company where they both worked. When it was discovered that they were going out together they were told that one of them must leave, since it was against company policy to have liaisons between male and female employees or to have married couples working for the concern. As you know, this used to be common policy among large Japanese companies and some still follow it. I often think about Noriko-san [another sister] and her unhappy experience at Hitachi (35).

Sometimes it seems that working for big companies can have certain benefits. Some companies let employees buy things at the company store at a discount. Women can take classes in flower arranging and the tea ceremony without having to pay, and the companies often have nice places where employees can go on vacation for very little money. But when I think about what happened to Noriko-san, I wonder about those big companies.

In fact, according to something I read lately, the classes in flower arranging and the tea ceremony are a holdover from the Meiji period (36). The big industry in the early days was textiles, and sixty to seventy percent of textile workers were women. To get workers, the industrialists often built factories close to villages. That way they could recruit sons and daughters (especially daughters) of people who were used to the old feudal ways. *Samurai* (37) were no longer *samurai* but they still controlled the government. Farmers paid their taxes in rice. When crops were bad, the poor farmers still had to turn over rice for taxes, even if their families went hungry, and if there was a daughter in the family she would have to go to work in the textile factory, or even be sold to the Tobita prostitute district in Osaka or the Yoshiwara district in Tokyo (38). The farmers really didn't have a lot of choice. Sending off the daughter meant *kuchiberashi* [one less mouth to feed]. To persuade the parents to let their children go to live and work in unfamiliar places, the factory owners built dormitories, they promised to provide healthy diets, and they assured the parents that all workers would receive physical, intellectual, and moral training. They promised that the young women would be taught domestic skills expected of wives to improve their marriageability. In fact, the young women worked from sunrise to sunset. They received no pay except for kimono fabric and sometimes second-hand kimonos and slippers, and they were fed so poorly that many died of tuberculosis and other diseases.

This was evidently the basis for the present-day relationship between employer and employee in most Japanese companies today. You probably know all this, and you know the labor-management relationship is very much like a family relationship — a kind of paternalism, I guess, but with close ties and strong feelings of loyalty. If a worker cannot handle an assignment, it is given to someone else; the original worker is not penalized any more than a backward child would fall out of favor in a family. The backward child gets just as much to eat as the other children and is loved just as much.

You wrote about the transit strike in New York last month and how all those millions of people had to get about on foot and bicycles and roller skates. Roller skates? Toshiro-san was amazed when you said that James-san could walk to his office in five minutes. Here, of course, we have our *shunki toso* [spring strike] that disrupts the trains and subways every year. The workers use it to bargain for bigger midyear bonuses. Their basic pay depends primarily on how long they have been with the railroad or whatever, just as it is in every company, just as it was when you were here.

That hasn't changed. And women are still looked upon as temporary employees. When times are bad the women are the first to be let go, even though they may be more competent than some men. In the short time that I spent working in an office, I saw some men who simply could not have managed if they had not had good women assistants. Some of the women told stories at lunch about supervisors who didn't seem to know what day it was, but most of us were only working until we got married so we didn't take it too seriously. Not many companies hire women for professional or managerial jobs, although that is beginning to change. What generally happens is that a woman comes out of high school or junior college, talks to a representative sent to her school by some company, and takes a clerical or production line job. She often has to sign an agreement that she will retire at a certain age, or when she gets married, or when she has her first child. These agreements are not legal but thousands of women sign them and feel bound by them. So a young woman typically works for five or six years, gets married, quits work, and raises a family. She may be rehired when her children are old enough for school, and she may work for the next twenty years, but when business falls off she will find that she is expendable. Men here have job stability; women do not.

I was interested in what you wrote about the difficulties American women seem to be having in getting an Equal Rights Amendment approved. That march in Washington last July must have been terrible with the weather so hot and muggy. I was fascinated to hear that so many men took part and I wish I could have seen the photographs you took (39). Of course we have had an Equal Rights Amendment since 1947 — May 5, 1947, to be exact (I looked it up). It has accomplished something, I think, in that it gives women solid legal grounds when they bring lawsuits charging discrimination. We consider the Equal Rights Amendment a gift from the Americans, and it is hard to believe that American women don't have one themselves. Isn't this the sixtieth anniversary of voting rights for women in America?

Our amendment says that it is against the law to discriminate by sex for political, social, or economic reasons, but of course those are just *tatemae* [principles], and what actually happens is usually quite different. Companies obviously continue to discriminate; when women bring legal action, the judges often find in their favor, citing the E.R.A. as the basis for their decisions. The Supreme Court here last year [actually in March 1979] dismissed an appeal by Nissan Motors in a case that went back to 1969. Nissan had a mandatory retirement age of fifty for women and fifty-five for men. A woman named Miyo Nakamoto of Tokorozawa City not far from here turned fifty and was told she must retire. She said that Nissan's policy violated the Equal Rights Amendment and decided to take the matter to court. A Committee to Support Nakamoto-san was organized, Nakamoto-san set up a study group, which included some men, and she expanded the committee to cover other forms of discrimination against women. The court ruled in 1971 that women at age fifty were not as physically capable as men of the same age, and that the Nissan policy was not unfair. Another court upheld that decision early in 1973, but in February 1973 the Tokyo District Court reversed the lower courts, saying that a majority of Japanese people did not believe that the difference in retirement age based on sex was rational. The District Court did not say that Nissan's policy violated the E.R.A.; it just said that up until about age sixty, men and women were about equal in terms of general working ability, and there was no difference based on sex. The company had argued that men are usually the main source of income for a family, that women are dependent upon men, and that women should go back to the home at a certain age. The court disagreed, the company appealed, and the Supreme Court, as I said, has just dismissed the appeal. It ruled that Nissan had to pay Miyo Nakamoto (who had just turned sixty) twelve million yen [about sixty thousand dollars] for five years' pay. Unfortunately, this doesn't mean that from now on all companies, or even Nissan for that matter, will have to treat men and women equally in terms of mandatory retirement age. It is just one isolated victory for one woman, but it should certainly help discourage discrimination based on sex. Anyway, let's hope so.

We have a Labor Standards Law based on the E.R.A. with specialized regulations to protect working women. It prohibits employment of women on night shifts, prohibits employers from hiring women for dangerous jobs, prevents them from hiring women to work in the mines, provides for maternity leave before and after childbirth, requires that companies provide nursing hours for new mothers in their employ, gives women time off when they are having their menstrual periods, and forbids companies from firing women who are on maternity leave. (I looked all of this up for you and found it quite interesting.) These provisions are all for the physical protection of women. In addition, the law requires that workers doing the same job receive the same pay, regardless of sex, and you know what a laugh that is.

You suggested that I look at the want-ads in the newspaper, and I was interested to hear that American newspapers are not allowed to say that a job is only for a man or only for a woman. It's certainly not that way here. Most of the want-ads for women are looking for women between the ages of twenty-five and thirty-five. For a woman over thirty-five, the openings are mostly in insurance sales, or for part-time work, or for jobs as housekeepers, cooks for dormitories, and the like. I understand that want-ads for women used to specify that the woman must have *yoshitanrei* [a beautiful appearance]. That is no longer the case, but the major companies still hire only single women, if they hire any women at all. Even the government employment office clearly discriminates against women. The form for women to fill out is pink, the form for men is white. (There's a third form, with blue lettering on white paper, for part-time jobs.)

Yoko-san and I have talked about this and she agrees that working for a Japanese company can be rough for a woman. She says that some of the trading companies [Mitsui, Mitsubishi, Sumitimo, C. Itoh, and Marubeni are the major ones] still insist that a single woman in their employ must live with her parents. I don't think working for a big company is anything for me, and the idea of selling cosmetics (I wrote about that in my last letter) looks quite promising. I'll write you more about that next time. This letter has been long enough.

Sachiko

11 *June*

Dear Chie,

Exciting news! No, I'm not going to have another baby. (That's what Mariko-san thought when I called Yonago and told her I had news. If I were a man and told her I had news she wouldn't have thought that was what I meant, I'm sure. Besides, I believe I've told you that Toshiro-san and I have decided not to have any more children.) The news is that I'm going into business. You may remember that I wrote to you about that line of herbal cosmetics. Well, I tried the skin cream (Tamiko-san's friend got it for me), and I liked it very much.

You know how sensitive my skin is; well, this Noevir cream didn't give me any trouble. I'm sending you a jar by airmail so that you can try it yourself.

This friend of Tamiko-san (Yumiko Tanaka is her name) told me that she had had trouble with her skin, too. Do you remember what I wrote you about the cosmetic industry scandal? Well, Tanaka-san said the problem was mostly with coal-tar dyes used in the products. She told me about *kokuhisho* [black skin syndrome]. I had read some stories in the papers about that, and it is really quite alarming, with new horror stories appearing all the time as the trial goes on at Osaka (40).

Yumiko Tanaka (Tamiko-san's friend) has followed all this so closely because she is a Noevir Lady, which is a lot better than being an Office Lady (41). Noevir is a new company and has been doing very well, partly, I suppose, because so many women now have doubts about products made by some of the older companies, including American companies. Tanaka-san told me about the man who started Noevir, Hiroshi Okura, and I found his story interesting, especially since it turns out that Okura-san was the one who introduced feminine hygiene douches to Japan. (Do you remember my writing to you about that?)

Actually, Okura-san started as a Defense Force air cadet after college and was a pilot for four years. In the spring of 1963, he got married and quit flying to start a business at Osaka importing aircraft parts. He did all right, but the market was limited so he began to think in terms of importing consumer goods. He had been to the United States as a pilot and had seen feminine hygiene products, including the douche, that did not exist in Japan. He asked a physician he knew about the douche and was told that it was a good idea, so in 1964, the year of the Tokyo Olympics, he went into business under the name J. H. Okura & Co. and began importing feminine douches from a Chicago company called Abbott Laboratories. (Have you heard of them?) The J. H. in the company's name were the initials of a friend who helped Okura-san. He also got help from Yasuo Murakami, a language school graduate who had worked for a big company but had quit in disgust because the company did not let employees use their own ideas or do anything but follow the company system. Murakami-san helped Okura-san get pharmacies to stock the Abbott douches, but Japanese women were not familiar with them and they just gathered dust on the shelves. In addition to the douches, Okura-san imported kitchen dishracks made by an American company called Rubbermaid. Neither of these efforts was spectacularly successful and Okura-san nearly went bankrupt. What saved him was a visit to a friend whose wife had a business selling Tupperware products. Are you familiar with Tupperware? He showed his friend's wife one of his Rubbermaid dishracks and she thought it could be sold through the Tupperware home party method. So at one of her Tupperware parties she demonstrated the dishrack and every woman wanted one. Toshiro-san says he can remember when Japanese houses had cement sinks with only cold water. His mother's hands got so cold that she used to drop the dishes and break them. He says that even in the 1960s the kitchen was always the darkest part of a Japanese house. Anyway, Okura-san told the women at the Tupperware party that a red, yellow, or blue dishrack would brighten up their kitchens. He didn't have enough to go round at the first party and had to go back to his warehouse for more.

That's how he began, with three housewives using three cars. Each day they would go to a different part of Osaka to hold Rubbermaid home parties, and pretty soon the women were making more money than their husbands. They didn't want to stop, even on Sundays (42), so Okura-san could not stop on Sundays, either. Within a few months, the women were making two or three times as much as their husbands, so the husbands quit their jobs to go into business with their wives, buying their own cars and selling Rubbermaid products themselves. The original three couples became distributors for Okura-san and recruited saleswomen. They bought the dishracks at six hundred yen each [about three dollars] and sold them for two thousand yen [about ten dollars]. Okura-san gave them thirty percent profit on everything they sold, and they, in turn, gave a little something to every housewife who organized a party for them. The husbands drove the cars, the wives did the selling, and the couples did so well that their neighbors, seeing them with good clothes and driving nice new cars, became curious. When they found out what was going on, some of them wanted to get into selling Rubbermaid products, too, so the original three couples became distributors. Their apartments became little warehouses, and they were forced to sleep in their kitchens because the other rooms were filled with merchandise. Okura-san himself was no longer doing any selling; he was busy as an importer and wholesaler, and he hired a truck to keep his distributors supplied with merchandise.

After a while, he realized that the Rubbermaid products took up so much space that it limited their profit potential. The douches he had imported were still in the warehouse, and he began thinking that perhaps he could use the sales force he had built up to sell douches as well as dishracks, and since the douches were much smaller they might be more profitable. The trunk of a car — Okura-san always used the largest size Toyota — could hold a lot more douches than dishracks, and since both sold at the same price a sales person could make a lot more money selling douches with no more effort, so there would be more incentive to sell douches than dishracks. Okura-san had given the Abbott Laboratories product a new name, using the English word "Confidence," but he was embarrassed about discussing the douche with women. He finally brought himself to mention it to one of the women who was now a Rubbermaid distributor. She wasn't sure that the douche could be sold at home parties the way dishracks were sold, but she wanted one for herself, especially after Okura-san told her what the doctor had said about the douche shortening a woman's menstrual period (which may or may not be true, by the way). The distributor told her salesladies about the douche and their reaction was the same as hers: they didn't know whether they could sell it, but each wanted to try it for herself. After a few weeks, the women all said they liked the product a lot and thought they could sell it, so Okura-san let them show the douche to women who came to Rubbermaid parties. It turned out to be even more popular than the dishrack, and Okura-san soon found himself picking up salesladies at nine-thirty each morning and taking them to locations, usually apartment complexes, where they would make sales at home parties, beginning at eleven-thirty. He began hearing from people all over Japan who wanted to be distributors for the item. So for two or three years there was a boom in douches. Many distributors bought or hired vans, put twenty salesladies into each van, and dropped them off in different neighborhoods each day to give home parties selling douches. A housewife who gave the party would get five or ten percent of the saleslady's take, and after each party the saleslady would make arrangements with one of the guests to have another party the following day at that woman's house or apartment. A saleslady would give three parties a day. Each guest would receive a pamphlet explaining the douche product, telling women not to be shy about discussing it, and pointing out that using the product was good for a woman's health. Cleanliness is the true beauty, the pamphlet said, and using the douche was something that every woman owed to her husband. Each of Okura-san's salesladies was soon selling two dozen douches per day while the distributors scouted new locations for parties. The salesladies received a forty percent commission, so a woman could earn nearly twenty thousand yen [about one hundred and twenty dollars] per day. Okura-san quickly exhausted his supplies and was forced to beg Abbott Laboratories to rush more stock to him. Orders came in from Korea and Taiwan, and Okura-san profited from these sales as well, while continuing to import aircraft parts.

Okura-san and his wife Etsuko counted the day's cash after dinner each evening (43), and sometimes they had to sit up until three or four in the morning before it was all counted. Then some Japanese companies started making douches and flooded the market. The Abbott Laboratories douche was guaranteed for three years, and the only new customers were newly-married women. Okura-san began looking about for something else with more possibilities for repeat business.

All this information, by the way, comes from a new book that has just been published here. It's called *Koibito no Kiseki* [*Miracle of Sweethearts*]. I wanted to tell you about the cosmetics business that Okura-san started, but Toshiro-san came in and I had to make sure his *furo* (44) was all right. I think I wrote earlier that he had given up smoking. He has not had a single cigarette since the first of the year; I understand that giving it up can be very difficult, and I'm so proud that he has done it — and very touched to think that he did it for me. He's soaking in the tub now, and I'll finish this up so I can drop it in the mailbox at the corner. I knew Toshiro-san would be working late, and I was glad to have time to write to you at some length. Next time I'll tell you about the cosmetics. Everything is going well and I'm really very excited about it.

Sachiko

7 July

Dear Chie,

Can you believe that after three weeks I have recovered my initial investment in the cosmetic business and, in fact, have a little more besides? Toshiro-san is working late again, so I have time to tell you more about Okura-san and Noevir (that's the name of the cosmetic line I'm selling), but first I should fill you in on the election we had last month. The turnout was the highest in twenty-two years, with 74.5 percent of eligible voters going to the polls, and Fusae Ichikawa [*see* note 1] not only got re-elected to the *Sangiin* [upper house of the Diet] but won more votes than anyone else. Still, only fourteen members of the *Sangiin* are women, and a lot of them are celebrities like Chinatsu Nakayama, who is an actress, a singer, a writer, and the youngest woman ever elected. The *Shugiin* [lower house] has only nine women members.

I told you in my last letter about Tamiko-san's friend Yumiko Tanaka, the Noevir Lady. My original intention was to become a Noevir Lady myself, and I talked with Tanaka-san's distributor, but then I thought it over and decided to become a sales representative, or distributor, instead. That required an investment of one hundred thousand yen [about five hundred dollars] for the *hoshokin* [security money], and I had saved a little more than that from my typing work so I used it to get off to a good start. Toshiro-san is not too happy about this. He doesn't like the idea of my working and he doesn't think I'll be very successful. I certainly didn't tell him that some Noevir distributors — even some Noevir Ladies — made more money than their husbands; he might not like the idea of my earning more than he, although that's not anything I really expect to happen. I'm what they call a Number Two representative, and I have to recruit one hundred and fifty Noevir Ladies. So far I have six, and I expect to get another four within a week or so.

◇51

Yoko-san and Tamiko-san have both been very helpful. In fact it was Tamiko-san's idea that I bake a cake and let her give a tea party for some of her friends at which I could explain what I was doing and see if any of them were interested. It went very well, and several of the women said they definitely wanted to be Noevir Ladies. A few others seemed interested and at least some of them will probably decide to come along. Yoko-san has to work during the day, but she gave a party one evening last week and invited some of her friends. They were just as interested as Tamiko-san's friends, and I realized that what has worked for Okura-san at his home parties was working for me. I guess you'd call it *gunshushinri* [crowd psychology]. In Okura-san's case, one woman bought a dish-rack or a douche or some cosmetics and the others wanted to buy. In my case, one woman decided to become a Noevir Lady and the others thought it might be a good idea.

What I like so much about working for Noevir, beside the money, is that these cosmetics are really safe, and women appreciate that. I wrote to you about the scandal in our cosmetic industry. Well, women here are very much aware of that and are looking for products they can trust. The Noevir line is more expensive than some, including Avon, but is not so expensive as others, such as Pola and Shiseido. Price doesn't seem to be a big issue, my Noevir Ladies tell me. Customers are just so grateful to discover products that won't give them trouble after what they have been through, or at least read about, with other cosmetics.

The unusual thing about Noevir cosmetics is that they contain no artificial ingredients, not even as preservatives. The fats and oils are natural fats and oils, including shark liver oil from Australia and oil from the jojoba plant that grows in Arizona. You wrote that you had taken photographs of the Pueblo Indians in Arizona, so maybe you have seen jojoba plants. The Noevir products also contain fatty acids from soybeans, beeswax from Africa, and sixteen different herbal extracts from West Germany. In fact, Okura-san originally got into the business by importing cosmetics from West Germany.

I wrote to you about Okura-san's earlier businesses importing aircraft parts and merchandising Rubbermaid dishracks and Abbott feminine hygiene douches. When the douche business fell off in 1970, he began handling some imported foods. Then he imported some West German containers very much like Tupperware, but the fact that items like those last so long meant that the market was limited. Okura-san was on the lookout for disposable items that would provide a lot of repeat business, preferably items for women, so he studied merchandising methods used to sell cosmetics. When he saw how many different brands of cosmetics were struggling to compete, he was naturally discouraged. He realized that unless a newcomer had something new and unique to offer, it would be extremely difficult to enter the market.

An advertisement in an American magazine for some herbal cosmetics gave him his inspiration. He had seen wild herbs such as thyme, sage, fennel, and rosemary growing in the mountains and was excited about the idea of cosmetics made from such natural plants. He wrote to the American company that he would like to import the line and sell it in Japan, but the company said it did not make enough for export. So he wrote to some European cosmetic companies, asking them if they made herbal cosmetics. He had a list of top companies and secondary companies which he had obtained by writing to various foreign embassies and consulates in Tokyo and asking for the names of cosmetic companies in the countries they represented. Eventually, he heard from a West German company called Friebird in Baden Baden, a name supplied to him by the German Chamber of Commerce in Tokyo. The Friebird people said they had checked with the plastics company which made food containers, they heard that Okura-san had a reputation for effective selling, and they would be happy to do business with him. So Okura-san went to the German Embassy in Tokyo and told the Germans that he was interested in importing German merchandise for sale in Japan. He said that he wanted the best possible interpreter provided for him in Germany, and the Germans were very cooperative.

He flew to Frankfurt, was met at the airport by his interpreter, rented a car, and drove south along the Rhine through Heidelberg and all the way to Karlsruhe, at the northern edge of the Black Forest, the Schwarzwald. He stopped there and went to a cosmetic shop, where he saw a good many herbal cosmetics on sale. I don't know how much of this to believe, but he said later that he saw many women with beautiful skin in Karlsruhe. At Baden Baden, he was received by the people at the Friebird Company and shown barrels and barrels of herbal extracts. It was explained to him how the company mixed the various extracts to create its cosmetic products.

Okura-san contracted with the Friebird people to sell their products in Japan, and he placed an initial order for ten million yen [about fifty thousand dollars] worth of cosmetics, conditional on his obtaining an import license. He was afraid there might be problems in getting permission from the Japanese Department of Health and Welfare, but he got help from a chemist he met who showed the government people that the German products were safe and effective. He got the import license, the cosmetics arrived by air, and the first order was sold within a week, using the same home party techniques that had been so effective before.

The trouble was that after paying the high import duty and the air freight there wasn't much profit, so Okura-san decided to switch to sea freight. Unfortunately, the Suez

Canal had been shut since the 1967 war in the Middle East, so it took seventy days for the merchandise to reach Japan. The cosmetics had deteriorated en route and were worthless. Okura-san lost fifty million yen [about two hundred and fifty thousand dollars] in that disaster. His chemist friend, Kazunari Suzuki, was more than just sympathetic. He suggested to Okura-san that he might be able to import just the extracts from Germany and manufacture his cosmetics in Japan.

I'll have to save the rest for another letter. I haven't yet run the water for Toshiro-san's *furo*, and he should be coming home shortly, so I had better stop now. You know how long it takes to heat the water. I wouldn't want Toshiro-san to think I was derelict in my wifely duties now that I'm a business lady.

Sachiko

26 *July*

Dear Chie,

Thank you for your good wishes. I now have more than two dozen Noevir Ladies, the business is going along nicely. Tamiko-san and Yoko-san are impressed. They never believed that I would be so successful, and frankly I'm rather surprised myself. Even Hajime seems to sense that I am happier and busier, although I still get him ready for school every morning and am home by the time he returns from his *juku* class before dinner.

What has helped me recruit Noevir Ladies is my P.T.A. work. When nobody wanted to put out the monthly bulletin, I volunteered, and that way I got to meet a lot of people. Since this is a new community, most people don't know each other the way they do in an older community, so many women are eager to make friends. When I mentioned to some mothers that they could give home parties and sell Noevir products, I pointed out that it was a good way to meet people as well as to make extra money. The company trained me in how to apply makeup, and now I train my Noevir Ladies. You should see me.

You ask about the safety of the cosmetics, and your point about natural things not always being safe is well taken. I remember your writing about the agonies you suffered after peeling that mango and after touching poison ivy. (We don't have poison ivy in Japan, but we have other things.) A few women evidently are sensitive to the herbs used in Noevir cosmetics (I asked the wholesaler about that), but I gather there are relatively few complaints, and so far I have not heard any, even from women who had had troubles with other cosmetics.

You also asked whether I had met Okura-san and how I knew so much about him. No, I have not met him, and what I know has come mostly from the wholesaler (who does know him) and from the book I mentioned in my last letter. They say that he was always very enterprising. At college, he devoted more time to mountain climbing than to his engineering studies, and he started an Alpine club. When he found that the college would not give his club any financial aid, he solved the problem by supporting a friend who was a candidate for the presidency of the student organization. Okura-san went to all the college sports clubs and promised them that if his friend got elected he would use his influence as president of the student organization to get them financial support. The friend did win the election and he did obtain financial aid for the Alpine club and the other sports clubs.

He has a history of planning everything out very carefully in advance. When he decided to climb a mountain in winter without a tent, he first spent months studying the conditions he would face. The planning was worthwhile. He had to endure all sorts of hardships on the climb, but he made it even when everybody said it was impossible.

In Osaka there's an organization, really a sort of social club, that gives men and women from respectable families a chance to meet. It's called Natsugi, after the town of Nishinomiya City, near Osaka, and Okura-san was introduced to Natsugi in 1962 or '63 after he made his first visit to America. It was there that he met Etsuko. Her maiden name was Morimoto, she was the eldest of three daughters, she came from Kobe, and she was working as an Office Lady in the export department of a textile company. They were married six months later; she was twenty-three, he was twenty-seven. I don't know how carefully that was planned; I'm sure some things in life are determined by fate, like you and James-san meeting in Bucharest, and there is nothing we can do to direct the hand of fate. I certainly didn't plan to sell Noevir cosmetics, yet it looks like I'm going to make a success of it.

The Natsugi club where Okura-san met Etsuko Morimoto is also where he met Kazunari Suzuki, the chemist I mentioned in my last letter who helped Okura-san get permission to import those Friebird cosmetics from West Germany. Suzuki-hakase [Dr. Suzuki] was employed as a researcher by the Club Cosmetic Company, an old and well regarded concern that had practically gone bankrupt in 1954 after more than fifty years in business. A man named Nakayama was the head of the company; he had not been able to keep up with new ideas as the Japanese changed their tastes after the war, in cosmetics as in so many other things, and had barely been able to keep Club Cosmetic going. Nakayama-san still paid a salary to Suzuki-hakase, perhaps hoping that he could revive the company and would need a chemist.

Okura-san had found another West German company (It's called Drago) that would export herbal extracts, but he needed someone to manufacture cosmetics from the extracts. One day he received a telephone call from Suzuki-hakase, who said he had spoken with Nakayama-san. Club Cosmetic's old brick factory was idle; perhaps it could be put back into operation. Okura-san went to look and found vagrants sleeping in the doorway of the place. The plant had been bombed during the war and had never been properly repaired. The roof leaked, there were holes in the floor, the machinery looked antique. Still, if Nakayama-san and his old partners in Club Cosmetic would go fifty-fifty with him in putting up the necessary capital, Okura-san would go into business with them. Nakayama-san said they didn't have that kind of money, and it looked like there would be no deal, but while discussing the possibilities at the plant, Okura-san looked into the backyard and saw a large heap of empty bottles marked Cologna Flouveil 70. Club Cosmetic Company was marking its seventieth anniversary in 1973, and the bottles had been made to celebrate the anniversary. Okura-san realized that if they could use the old bottles they could at least save the cost of new containers, so he arranged with Nakayama-san to start the Flouveil Company, a sister company to Club Cosmetic, and to have Club Cosmetic produce a skin moisturizer that could be sold in the cologne bottles under the name Flouveil 70. This was in 1973. Using the home party technique that had been so successful with the Rubbermaid dishracks, the Abbott Laboratories feminine hygiene douches, and the Friebird cosmetics from West Germany, Okura-san marketed Flouveil 70 skin moisturizer and built up a sales organization with hundreds of Flouveil *biyoshain* [beauty consultants], as he called them.

After a few years, the old Club Cosmetic Company had put its financial troubles behind it and was doing very well. Nakayama-san should have been happy. Instead, he started making demands on Okura-san, saying that he should have more than half the company stock since the products carried the Club Cosmetic name. People were saying that Club Cosmetic had come back from the edge of bankruptcy only through Okura-san's initiative, and Nakayama-san evidently felt that he was losing face. Okura-san refused Nakayama-san's demand. He said that the success of Flouveil cosmetics had come from the fact that herbal cosmetics were a fresh idea. He had pioneered in marketing herbal cosmetics in Japan, the sales success was based on methods he had used to market other products, and he knew how to apply those methods to selling cosmetics. Nakayama-san insisted that Okura-san could not have achieved his success without the Club Cosmetic foundation on which to build, and he demanded that a new contract be drawn up stating that the old company would be responsible for production, promotion, and publicity, with Okura-san responsible only for marketing. It had been decided that Club Cosmetic would introduce a new line of products for men, but the old crowd at Club announced one day that it had decided not to proceed with the men's line and that it was raising wholesale prices without notice. Okura-san would have to take a smaller mark-up or raise the prices he charged consumers.

Okura-san was furious, and there was a big argument. Nakayama-san said that he could no longer deal with Okura-san, that Okura-san would have to sell his shares in the company. Okura-san asked Nakayama-san to sell him the brand name Flouveil. Nakayama-san agreed, but he asked an enormous price. If Okura-san could not pay, he said, then he had better sell his shares in the company and get out. Club Cosmetic people meanwhile were selling Flouveil 70 to wholesalers, bypassing Okura-san. Since Okura-san had no rights to the trademark he had worked to build up, he realized that he could not win and decided to withdraw. He had promised one hundred and twenty saleswomen and wholesalers a trip to Saipan as a reward for their efforts, and he went ahead with the trip, not telling anyone about his troubles with Nakayama-san. Not wanting to see any of them hurt, he made a deal with Nakayama-san: Club Cosmetic would retain the sales force after Okura-san's departure.

I don't know whether or not you like stories like these about battling businessmen. In some ways the men behave like squabbling schoolboys. On the other hand, very large amounts of money are involved and all of us depend, finally, on economic conditions that determine the fortunes of business, and I guess it's businessmen's decisions — good or bad — that help shape economic conditions.

Oh, dear. I had no idea it was so late. The story of how Okura-san went on to start Noevir will have to wait until my next letter, I'm afraid. Toshiro-san and Hajime will be home soon from the zoo and I must prepare dinner. I wish they could spend more time together; except for Sunday, Hajime hardly sees his father all week. At least there is Sunday. Some fathers play golf on Sundays and almost never see their children.

Sachiko

16 August

Dear Chie,

Your letter arrived yesterday and I am happy to hear that your picnic in Central Park went so well. As you describe all those thousands of people sitting on the grass and listening to the Philharmonic concert I get quite a different impression of New York from the one that all the stories about crime and squalor gave me. The fireworks must have been spectacular. Did that have something to do with the presidential election campaign?

You say that there is some Japanese-language television programming on one of the smaller TV stations, and I find that quite amazing. Is there really a large enough audience? I heard somewhere that several of the big hotels in Tokyo have television sets with one channel that has programs dubbed in English, and there is an English language radio station. We have always had American TV progams dubbed in Japanese, but Japanese programs in New York? I can hardly believe it, especially when you say that they sometimes come directly from Tokyo by satellite.

We watch quite a lot of television here, although I don't have much time for it anymore. According to a story in the newspaper the other day, ninety-three percent of Japanese people watch television at least once a day, and the average viewing time per person is three hours and nineteen minutes. If that is the average, you know some people must watch for more than twice that long. The average for housewives is nearly five hours, according to the newspaper, and that may be one reason why women here are generally better informed than men, although the newspaper didn't say that.

In addition to television cooking classes, they now have TV lessons in things such as flower arrangement, calligraphy, and the tea ceremony. Tamiko-san says they are very good. She also tells me that women send in poems that they have written after watching certain programs. The TV stations have the poems screened by teachers, who make comments that help the women improve their writing. There are quite a few voluntary study groups that use television for social and cultural education, and more than eighty percent of the participants are women. My own feeling is that the kind of woman they show in the television movies tends to be the sweet little wife trying to help her husband, or the dependable mother, or the lively young girl — types that our society accepts easily and that fit into the stereotype of the Japanese woman. The heroine in a dramatic story is always resigned as she endures the plot conflict. I guess that is supposed to make women viewers feel more content with their own, less dramatic lives.

My business is going along well, and guess who wants to be a Noevir Lady? I think I wrote to you once about Kazuko Fukuda, the woman who lives down the hall and who told me she had spent a whole afternoon playing *pachinko*. Well, she did fairly well selling life insurance, she's quite attractive, and I think that perhaps she could be a good Noevir Lady. True, she doesn't have any children, and she might even be divorced (She has never told me). In the beginning, Hiroshi Okura did not like the idea of having divorcées as Noevir Ladies. They did not fit his ideal of what a Noevir Lady should be. Now he has evidently seen that divorcees can be good salesladies, too. Fukuda-san is attractive (She could be thirty-two or fifty-two — I really have no idea), she has a pleasant manner, she seems motivated to make money, and I don't see why she couldn't do just as well as any of my other Noevir Ladies. After all, the products are good, women like them, and it just takes a little friendly woman-to-woman talk to persuade someone that she should try a Noevir skin cream or moisturizer or whatnot. If Fukuda-san does as well as my other Noevir Ladies have been doing, she will do quite well indeed, and — since I receive a percentage of whatever she takes in — so will I.

I wrote to you in my last letter about Okura-san having to leave Club Cosmetic Company. He sold his stock in the company to Nakayama-san and others so he had quite a lot of money — five hundred and forty million yen [about two million seven hundred thousand dollars, and Japan has no capital gains tax], according to what I have heard, although that may be an exaggeration. He had recruited most of the people in the company and had taught them the business, so when he announced his resignation at the Nagasaki branch, almost everybody in the office burst into tears and begged him to start a new company. The same thing happened at Tokyo, at Nagoya, and at the main office in Osaka. A lot of people said that if Okura-san resigned, so would they, because their loyalty was more to him than to the company.

According to the new book about Okura-san and Noevir, there was once a famous businessman named Yasuzaemon Matsunaga who, when he met another businessman, would always ask him if he had ever had a serious setback. That, he said, was the only way a businessman could learn. Okura-san took comfort from the experience of another businessman, Seiichi Suzuki, who started a wax company during the war, built it up after the war was over, and in 1962 made a deal with a big American wax company. The American company was S. C. Johnson of Racine, Wisconsin. Maybe you've heard of it. Well, Suzuki-san's ideas did not fit those of the American management and he had to withdraw from the deal and resign. One year later, he started a new company called Duskin and he has been very successful, using women sales representatives just the way Okura-san has done. Okura-san figured that if Suzuki-san could do it, so could he. In his final speech at the main office of Club Cosmetic Company, he said that a successful businessman did not blame his troubles on anyone else. He might have lost the company and lost some money, he said, but even if he were dropped in the middle of the African desert he would be able to find a way to survive. He vowed to emerge from his difficulties and to be successful once again.

Okura-san still had the J. H. Okura Company and decided to manufacture cosmetics under that name. In July 1978 he changed the name of J. H. Okura Company to Noevir Co., Ltd. and made a deal with the Drago people in West Germany to import the herbal extracts. Starting with twenty million yen [about one hundred thousand dollars] in capital, he began to build a line of Noevir skin creams, skin lotions, moisturizers, facial cleansers, and foundations, that he hoped would grow to include face powder, lipsticks, rouge, eye shadow, nail enamel, cologne, perfume, hair conditioners, soaps, and shampoos. People who had worked for Flouveil came to him and asked if they could work for Noevir, not so much because of any dissatisfaction with Flouveil as because they were excited about the prospect of being involved in a new venture with a man they could respect. One woman told him that Nakayama-san was too conservative, that he thought good products could sell themselves. She felt that Okura-san was more aggressive. Another woman said that Okura-san used some methods that were very American and had actually imported some American products as well as American merchandising techniques, but that he still had traditional Japanese ideas. A young man said that he could learn a lot about business from Okura-san. Each one had his or her own reasons for wanting to join Okura-san, and when the chemist Kazunari Suzuki (no relation to the Duskin Suzuki) left Flouveil to join him, bringing along a laboratory team, Okura-san was ready to move. With a sales force and a laboratory, he could compete with anyone.

Well, in eight months Noevir had seven thousand women working as Noevir Ladies (I guess he borrowed the name from Avon Ladies) and sales representatives [distributors]. One woman in Chiba Prefecture had sales of one million yen [about ten thousand dollars] per month within two months, and she had never had any selling experience before. A neighbor had sold her some Noevir skin lotion the way Tamiko-san's friend Yumiko Tanaka sold some to me, she liked the product just as I did, and she started selling Noevir products herself, just as I did except that she started as a Noevir Lady and I started as a distributor.

Another woman had been been a retail clerk in Mitaka City [part of Tokyo] selling on commission and making very little money. A woman she did not know called on her and sold her a bottle of Noevir skin lotion; the woman came back in a few weeks and asked her opinion of the product. Nobody had ever done that before and she was so impressed she decided to become a Noevir Lady herself. As a matter of fact, I think she started as a distributor, the way I did.

Maybe Okura-san does have some traditional Japanese ideas, but putting the company ahead of the individual is not part of his thinking. He says it's foolish to work for the company. You should have your own personal objectives and work for yourself to attain those objectives. Nobody else can do it for you; you have to do it for yourself. In fact, Okura-san discourages the hiring of women who have worked on a salary basis in jobs that got them accustomed to receiving regular paychecks. He says that tends to make people complacent, whereas he is looking for more aggressive people. One can be aggressive and still appear gentle and smiling, the way people expect a woman to be, and I have found that that is still the most effective manner for a woman to have. It turns out that only half the women who apply to be representatives, like me, are accepted. I don't know if it's still true, but in the beginning Okura-san insisted that Noevir Ladies and representatives be married women with young children. He didn't want divorcées, because he said a busy salesperson needed a husband who understood what she was doing and was supportive. The husband had to have a stable job, too. Okura-san reasoned that in our society young mothers have more incentive to work because they want their children to have good educations and they want their families to have better homes and more luxuries. He could have been talking about me, so while I guess somebody might say he's using women and the nature of Japanese society to his own advantage, I can't say that I mind. Nor do I think that Fukuda-san should be disqualified because she has no children and might even be a divorcée.

I haven't mentioned all this to Toshiro-san. If he ever got ideas about putting his own interests ahead of his company's interests it might be disastrous for him, so I don't want to put those ideas into his head. He would probably laugh at me, anyway. He has been brought up to think in a certain way, as I guess most of us are, and for a lot of Japanese men it is not a bad way to think. For Japanese women, it's another story. I think Okura-san is absolutely right. The odds are so high against a woman succeeding in a Japanese company that women like me are much better off working on their own the way I am doing.

Of course Toshiro-san has no idea how much money I am making from my business, and he has the satisfaction of knowing that all of our household expenses come out of his salary. A man needs that, I think. It will be rather extraordinary for him when he discovers that he has a wife who is becoming financially independent.

Sachiko

4 September

Dear Chie,

Last year we took only three days' vacation because Toshiro-san did not want to be away from the office for any longer than he could help. This year it was I who was too busy and I'm afraid poor Hajime had to spend his vacation without his mother. He did get a nice vacation, though, and so did Tamiko-san's boys Ken and Tadashi. As you know, everything during the summer is booked far in advance, but there are modest-priced lodgings at Kujukuri, the beach in Chiba Prefecture, that had some vacancies at the end of the season. I treated Tamiko-san, her two boys, and Hajime to a few days at Kokuminshukusha — that's the name of the inn — and they all enjoyed it enormously. Hajime is a little young, perhaps, but you know how boys are at that age. He just worships his older cousins, so it was a great pleasure for him to be in their company for a few days and Tamiko-san says he didn't give her a bit of trouble. You should have seen how suntanned and excited he was when he came home, bringing some seashells as a gift for me.

A few months ago I had more time than I knew what to do with. Now I have more money and less time. The real problem is that Toshiro-san is uncomfortable about my having so many cartons of merchandise in the apartment. I am going to have to find an office in order to have room for my stock and to have a place where I can meet with my Noevir Ladies without worrying about the house being in order. It is not easy to keep house and run a business as well. There was one day when Hajime wasn't feeling well, and my Noevir Ladies were bringing in their monthly revenues, I had to have all my paperwork finished so that I could turn the money over to my wholesaler by the end of the month, and for a while there I didn't know what I was going to do. Dinner wasn't ready when Toshiro-san got home, he was tired, and he was rather upset. He is accustomed to having everything just so, and it was the first time that I had ever failed to have dinner prepared on time. Hajime and Toshiro-san are both feeling better now and the crisis is over. A man has only one job. A woman finishes her work in the evening and then has to start a second job, which is about the same for women all over the world, I guess.

I suppose I really should be grateful for the fact that so many Japanese women do not work, or work only part-time, because that means women are home when my Noevir Ladies call on them. I should also be grateful that the Japanese tradition of having the woman of the house control the family's finances is still alive and well. That means a woman can buy Noevir cosmetics without having to account to her husband for how she has spent the money. Of course I now have money of my own, and quite a lot even after paying all my business expense, but even when Toshiro-san was the only one making money I was the one who decided how it would be spent. You really should persuade James-san to turn those things over to you. He must have enough to do with that history of the world he has put together. It sounds fascinating and I'm glad that you were able to translate some books for him so that he was able to include so much Japanese history. I hope his book is selling well.

Toshiro-san is very excited about the fact that his company, and specifically his division, has just won a Deming Prize For Application (45). When James-san was here he mentioned that he had met Dr. Deming (Toshiro-san was very impressed) so he can tell you about the Deming Prize. It really means a lot, and since quality control is Toshiro-san's speciality, and since all the top men in the division know how much he had to do with the company winning the award, it should be very helpful to his career.

Husbands of some Noevir representatives have quit their jobs and gone into business with their wives, you know. They saw how well their wives were doing and decided to join them. The most successful Noevir wholesaler, or at any rate one of the most successful, is a woman in Fuji City, Shizuoka Prefecture. Her name is Eiko Inaba and in 1973 she married a man with whom she had grown up in Fuji City. He was training to be a cook and two years later they started a *tonkatsu* [deep-fried pork chop] shop. They had a helper in the restaurant but she had to work from ten in the morning until three in the afternoon, and then from five in the evening until ten at night. It was hard work and she never liked it. Then her husband caught cold, the virus got into his spine, he was in and out of the hospital, and it was impossible to keep the *tonkatsu* shop going. A friend suggested that she become a Flouveil distributor and she did. She started in 1975 and found that it was easy to sell Flouveil cosmetics because the press had been giving other cosmetics such bad publicity. She hired six friends as Flouveil *biyoshain*, although she had never had any selling experience, and neither had most of the others. One had sold another line of door-to-door cosmetics. Eiko-san asked to be taken along so that she could see how the woman approached prospective customers. Whatever technique she used it was evidently successful, or maybe the products sold themselves. Anyway, Eiko-san had sales of three million yen [about fifteen thousand dollars] in her first month, and after two or three months her husband joined her in the business. They had a two-and-a-half year old child, and the husband drove the car and took care of the child during the day while Eiko-san and the other ladies made their rounds. They would start knocking on doors in different parts of town at ten each morning and work until three in the afternoon. It was much easier than working in the *tonkatsu* shop, and it certainly paid better.

After four or five months, Eiko-san began taking on additional Flouveil *biyoshain* while some in her first group went off on their own, buying from her and selling to customers. In less than two years, Eiko-san was a wholesaler, and her first six Flouveil *biyoshain* had become Flouveil distributors. By the time Okura-san started Noevir in July 1978, Eiko-san had twelve hundred Flouveil *biyoshain* working through her six distributors. When she explained to everyone that Suzuki-hakase had moved from Flouveil to Noevir, she had no trouble persuading the Flouveil distributors and Flouveil *biyoshain* to become Noevir representatives and Noevir Ladies.

Of course Toshiro-san is not a *tonkatsu* cook and does well in what he is doing. In fact, now that his division has won the Deming Prize he has been busier than ever. He tries to get home for dinner two or three times a week, but he rarely does, which disappoints Hajime and disappoints me, too.

Sachiko

9 *November*

Dear Chie,

So sorry not to have written in all these weeks. The fact is, my little business has been growing and has kept me terribly busy. My only chance to relax is Sunday, and Sundays have been full of activities with Hajime and Toshiro-san, mostly baseball — like the Little League you have there. This has been Hajime's great passion lately. He is quite a good hitter and base-runner and would have been playing today except that it's raining, so his father took him to one of those outer space movies. It was nothing I wanted to see, so the rain gives me a chance to write.

You said something in your last letter about someone you knew at *Ms.* magazine having her infant son at the office with her (47). That is extraordinary, and I wonder how many American offices permit it. As you know, most Japanese women have always stopped working when they had children, although that is beginning to change. Some companies still require young women to retire when they get married, or at age thirty, even though that has been ruled unconstitutional. I think I once wrote to you about that. We had a case here a few years ago involving four women in the marketing promotion department of *Shufunotomo* (48). They were all in their thirties, two of them had children, and they were told that they would have to give up their office jobs and do field work. They had been clerks at *Shufunotomo* for an average of fifteen years each; now they would have to be out in the field each day promoting books and magazines and attending sales meetings. Every day would be different, and the women would not be able to count on getting home at a given hour each evening. The field work had always been done by men, and the women wondered why they were suddenly be assigned to these jobs. They could only conclude that the company wanted them to retire. One of the women did retire after the new work affected her health. Another woman had a miscarriage but did not quit. When the women complained to their union, they were told that the matter could not be discussed on a union-management level. The union said it was simply a problem for women, but a special women's department in the union agreed to support the *Shufunotomo* clerks, especially after one of them quit. After one year, *Shufunotomo* transferred the three remaining women back to their office jobs.

There was a case last year in Yokohama involving a woman who refused to quit her job after having a child. I saw something about it in the newspapers but I don't know how it came out. Actually, the case began in 1969. The woman's name was Shuko Tatenaka. She was a clerk at the Toyo Company, and she was the first woman in the company's history who had continued to work after having a child. Most women in the company had always retired after marriage, much less continuing to work after childbirth. The company said that a woman with a child functioned at only fifty percent of her capacity, as if that were some kind of scientific fact. The head of personnel, in fact, had told her when she married that a woman's happiness was in the home. He advised her to retire. Her husband was active in the union, and the company transferred him from Yokohama to Kyoto, despite his efforts to fight the transfer. His wife remained at Yokohama, and after two years he was able to return to Yokohama himself.

Under the 1947 law, a Japanese working woman who has a baby is entitled to twelve weeks' unpaid maternity leave — six weeks before the child is born and six weeks after. If the child comes later than expected, the leave can be extended, and a woman cannot be discharged during maternity leave (49). American women must have some similar sort of legal protection, don't they (50)? Anyway, when Shuko Tatenaka took maternity leave, she was again advised to retire. A woman, she was told, should concentrate on nursing her child. After her child was born, she was told that the company had no place for her except as a cook at the company dormitory. She took the case to the Yokohama District Court, she won, but the company appealed, and she lost in the appeals court. The company argued that a woman's ability to work was greatly reduced during the first year after childbirth because she had to nurse her infant and could not give all her energies to her job. Tatenaka-san had been given a job that suited her limited capability, the company said; to have done otherwise would have been discriminatory against male employees. A lot of organizations rallied to her cause, and there was a Committee to Support Tatenaka-san, but as I said, I don't know how it all came out.

I do know that I never thought much about all this until I got into business and stopped being just a comfortable housewife. The way I feel now, if Tatenaka-san did not win her case, the court was not following the precedent set in the early seventies. The case there involved a woman named Kazumi Suenami who got her job back at Mitsui Shipbuilding Company. That was after a battle that lasted nearly five years. I suppose it could be argued that Suenami-san's case was different, since she was sent a retirement notice on the fourth day of her maternity leave, which clearly violates the 1947 law. But isn't the same principle involved? Mitsui Shipbuilding said that a woman should retire when she got married. If a woman wished to continue working after marriage, she could, but only if she passed an ability test and only until she gave birth to her first child. Suenami-san wanted to keep working after her child was born, so she talked to women in her district. They organized a Committee to Support Suenami-san and adopted a slogan, "We Want Our Jobs to Continue After Childbirth." Members of the committee spoke at a conference of the national organization of Japanese mothers and at a conference of working women. The Osaka District Court ruled in December 1971 that Mitsui Shipbuilding could not force Suenami-san to give up her job after childbirth, but it took her until November 1973 to get her old job back.

A lot more mothers would work, I'm sure, if there were not such a shortage of good day care centers. You asked about that, and I tried to get some information for you, but the latest figures I could find were not too recent. As of October 1974, there were 7,342 day care centers and they could accommodate one and a half million infants and children. Nearly two years earlier, in December 1972, the Ministry of Health and Welfare said that parents of 2,420,000 children were looking for day care centers, so the demand was far greater than the supply, and I'm sure it still is. The city day care center here in Omiya is open from eight-thirty in the morning until five in the afternoon and is free for people on welfare. Others pay according to their income; the fee goes up to forty-nine thousand yen [about two hundred and forty-five dollars] per month for an infant, up to ¥ 28,600 [about one hundred and forty-three dollars] for a child under age three, and up to ¥ 16,960 [about $84.70] for a child from three to kindergarten age. A private kindergarten costs only fourteen thousand yen [about seventy dollars] per month, including two thousand yen [about ten dollars] for bus fares and fifteen hundred yen [about seven dollars and fifty cents] for lunches, but it's only open from nine o'clock until two.

What bothers me and a lot of other women is that even the existing day care centers are often unlicensed and unreliable. The operator of a day care center may charge thirty thousand yen a month [about one hundred and fifty dollars] but the children may be crowded into a rather small space and there is almost never a nurse. I have a friend whose son developed a fever at the day care center and it led to complications. The boy was left with a partial disability that might be permanent, although we all hope it can be overcome in time. That was one reason I did not want to return to work until Hajime was old enough for school and *juku*, and it's a reason why many young mothers would much rather work part time than have office jobs that give them less time to be with their children.

One of my Noevir Ladies, Reiko Sanda, has a son whose name is Hajime just like my son. She confided in me the other day that she was so happy to be working and to hear herself called by name for a change instead of being called *okusan* [wife] or *Hajime-chan-no-oka-a-san* [mother of Hajime]. Sanda-san confessed that she had never done anything, including having sex, except out of a sense of duty to her husband, that she had never felt entitled to do things because she wanted to, and that she had considered divorce. Now that she has returned to work, she feels more like a person in her own right and finds that her relationship with her husband has improved a good deal.

I gather that most countries did not take the United Nations Year of the Woman too seriously back in 1975, but Japan did. We issued a special postage stamp, and I found one in a drawer the other day. I'll try to remember to enclose it when I seal this letter. Labor unions here had traditionally taken the position that working women's problems were not relevant to the problems of working men but were something separate, so they did not back women union members in cases of sex discrimination. Big companies gave women a good chunk of retirement pay plus a bonus when they got married and quit work, so most women were happy to take the money and retire. How much they got depended on how long they had been working and how much they were making, but most got at least two hundred thousand yen [about one thousand dollars].

A company may not exactly have a policy of discrimination against women, but it is accustomed to having women retire at earlier ages than men. The excuse generally given is that women just do supportive work and do not contribute as much as men since their energies are divided and they cannot be as dedicated to the company's welfare as a man is. They have also argued that in most families the woman's wages are not the primary source of income, and they have used that as an excuse to pay women less than men for the same duties

(51). In addition, they have insisted on early retirement for women because they say women's jobs are mostly supportive, and they get less benefit from a woman's work than from a man's; yet a woman with a lot of seniority may receive more than a man who works hard and contributes a lot to the company, which would be unfair. Some women at Nissan Motor took their case to court, claiming that they had high technology jobs whereas other women had very simple jobs, and that if Nissan did not give women equal opportunities for jobs with a lot of responsibility, it was not the women's fault. The court upheld their claim, which surprised a lot of businessmen, I think.

The International Year of Women did get a lot of attention here. While the newspapers tried to laugh it off, women seized upon it as an opportunity to make some real social changes. You know how people are here. Something has to come up outside the country before we take any action. We don't so much act as react. That's how it was in this case. People who had never thought much about the situation of women in Japan began to talk about it. There were books on the subject, discussions in various organizations, conferences, newspaper articles, television talk shows, and magazine articles. I remember being quite involved at the time, and it must have been about then that I began to question a lot of things that I had always considered above question.

Some other factors were involved in the changes that began in 1975. For one thing, the oil shock forced a lot of companies to let people go, mostly women. The companies generally have basic policies as to who will be laid off first. It's usually men over fifty, women over thirty, women with husbands, employees who are not too bright or have physical shortcomings, and employees with high absentee rates. None of these were thought to contribute as much to the company as other employees. In 1949, according to a story I read, the average Japanese working woman worked for only 3.2 years before retiring. By 1975, she was working nearly six years before retiring, and many working women had no men to help support them. A lot of Japanese women now in their fifties never married because so many of their male counterparts died in the Pacific War. That must have been true in Russia and many European countries, too. It must happen after every war.

You and I were lucky to have been born a little too late to be in the generation of women that so far outnumbered men (52). We can only pray that Hajime, our nephews, and your step-sons never have to go to war. Or perhaps we had better just pray that there never will be another war. None of us would be spared in a nuclear war, and the international news is sometimes quite discouraging. So is the agitation on the part of some people here to change the Constitution so that we can have a military again instead of just a self-defense force.

Sachiko

26 December

Dear Chie,

We all went shopping in the Ginza [Tokyo's equivalent to New York's Fifth Avenue] last weekend and you never saw such crowds. What upset me and a lot of other women was the vulgar Christmas display put up by Matsuya [a big department store] — a huge poster, six stories high, showing a Western woman completely nude except for a red ribbon. The poster covered the entire interior wall of the store, and I think some women were as disturbed by the fact that the model was Caucasian as by the fact that she was nude. We Japanese women don't look like that, we are not built like that, and some people are so upset by all the Western models in Japanese advertising that someone has put up an ad in the subway showing a smiling Japanese woman who has just x-ed out some Western models wearing bikinis.

The prices in the stores are incredible. A woman's Burberry raincoat sells for one hundred and fifty thousand yen [about seven hundred and fifty dollars] and yet you see women everywhere with Burberry raincoats. I guess most of them are Office Ladies whose living expenses are low or women with rich husbands. Toshiro-san needs some new shoes and a good pair costs sixty thousand yen [about three hundred dollars]. I don't know where people get all the money.

Tamiko-san and her family have gone north to Kushiro [in Hokkaido] for a few days to visit Masanori-san's family (His father has not been well) and to see the cranes. Young Tadashi is very interested in birds, and the cranes have arrived much earlier than usual, which makes some people think that it must have got cold earlier in Siberia this year, or that there is less food available in areas where the cranes always stop on their migration to Kushiro. They said on television that there are more cranes now than ever. After the war, there were only three hundred left and it was feared that they might become extinct. Now they are protected by law, the farmers have helped them to survive, and some farmers in Kushiro regret this. They say that the government should either let them shoot the birds or should subsidize them for their crop losses. About thirty-five hundred cranes have arrived at Kushiro so far and they are expecting another thousand.

My business has kept me so busy that I was not able to do much about *susuharai* [traditional yearend housecleaning; *susu* means soot, *harai* comes from the noun *harau* meaning purification, and the term comes from the time when the Japanese used wood-burning stoves for cooking]. To make the apartment spotless for the new year, I had the maid come in two extra days. You wrote about working until midnight with our mother to prepare food for the New Year's Day visitors and hearing the nearby *joyano kane* [temple bell] chiming out the old year. Going to the Shinto shrine after midnight sounds lovely.

One of Hajime's little friends from school has a Christmas tree so we had to get him a little one. We haven't much space for it, so it had to be quite small. It does look pretty, even if it's not very Japanese. For Christmas, Hajime got electric trains, also very small, and he was ecstatic. I got Toshiro-san a handsome briefcase to replace his old one. Toshiro-san, Hajime, and I wish you and James-san a happy new year. It will have to be quite spectacular to outdo this past year so far as I'm concerned. As I have been writing you, things have certainly changed a lot for me since June, and the better I do with my business the more I think about the terrible waste of woman-power in the world, perhaps especially in Japan. Women can do so much when they are given the opportunity. Men may worry about that. They may fear that they will lose their jobs to women, but with the birthrate falling here and in so many other countries, I think the time is coming when the world will no longer be able to afford not to make more effective use of women.

There was a symposium at Nagoya earlier this month on women's image of life in the 1980s and a Swedish woman spoke. Her husband is the secretary of the Swedish Embassy in Tokyo and she is the head of some kind of labor education organization. The husband took care of their ten-month old baby while she made her speech, and people were evidently quite startled at that. He was asked to go up on the stage and reply to questions. When he was asked what he thought of Japanese men, he said that he didn't think they were so different from other men in Eastern countries except that they worked harder. His job gave him an opportunity to meet men in the Japanese education, transportation, and welfare ministries, he said, and it was his impression that the men worked so hard from morning until evening that they had very little time for their families. The decisions they made were perfectly rational and technically sound but seemed to be lacking in humanity. He said that humanism appeared to have a low priority in their thinking, and he ascribed it to the fact that the men never had time to establish good family relationships.

Toshiro-san and I know plenty of families in which the man comes home only to sleep. A lot of men work late to get overtime pay, sometimes deliberately putting things off until late in the day so that they will have to work late. With overtime, a young man can make a lot more money than a man whose base pay is higher because of seniority. Toshiro-san now eats downtown three or four nights a week and tries to reach the Omiya City station in time to catch the last bus, which leaves at ten o'clock. If he misses it, he has to take a taxi. At least I know that he is late only because he has to be and not because he is drinking with his colleagues the way some men do but I wish that Hajime had more opportunity to be with his father. I'm sure Toshiro-san is aware of how important that is, and I think one reason he stopped smoking (It has now been a whole year since he had a cigarette) was to set a good example for Hajime. His father was a typical older-generation Japanese man who never exchanged more than a few words with

Toshiro-san. He is determined not to let that happen in our family, and he wants to establish a real relationship with Hajime.

Some men in the company have teased Toshiro-san about his eagerness to get home to his *kaka denka* [her highness the wife], but he doesn't let it bother him and it doesn't seem to make people respect him any less.

They had a conference at Aichi in connection with the International Year of Women in 1975 and about two hundred women discussed Japanese marriage problems. One woman said that her husband worked for a medium-sized company, came home every evening at nine o'clock, had dinner, took a bath, watched a little television, and went to sleep. He had no time for his children and no time for his wife. She complained that Japanese couples did not have enough time to enjoy life together and said that working hours should be shorter. The eight-hour day is basic, but a person can work twice that long and many men do, even though the pay for night shift work is only twenty-five percent higher and a health examination twice a year is required under the law. You know as well as I do, of course, that a large part of the time men spend away from their families is not spent working. The companies encourage their employees to socialize together, so they may play *mahjong*, *shogi*, or *go* after work or may just go out drinking together. Some of the bigger companies even have swimming pools and gymnasiums. You wrote about the company baseball teams in Central Park. You may have forgotten that here the best professional sports teams are sponsored by companies like the *Yomiuri Shimbun* [*Yomiuri* newspaper]. Another woman at that conference pointed out that if men spent more time at home their wives would have to spend more time taking care of them and would not be able to attend conferences like the one at Aichi.

More recently, a newspaper survey showed that the average Japanese husband and wife talk for only two and a half minutes a day, and that the conversation consists mostly of the man saying, "Let's eat," or "I'm going to take my bath now," or "I'm going to sleep." Are American men like that? I know James-san is not, and I'm happy to say that if the newspaper survey is correct, then Toshiro-san is not typically Japanese. There were a lot of things that we didn't talk about before I got into business, but now that I tell him things about that he has begun to tell me things about his own work, and little by little I have seen our relationship change — for the better, I should add. Not that we just talk about business, but one thing leads to another and — well, you know how it is. Of course there are some evenings when I am so tired I don't feel like talking to anyone, not even to Hajime, and that makes it easier for me to understand how Toshiro-san feels sometimes. When I think about all those husbands coming home at midnight after a long train ride, I can see why so many of them have so little to say to their families.

Speaking of men, the men in this house are getting hungry again, so I will close with the hope that we will see each other again somehow, somewhere in the coming year.

Sachiko

Dear Chie,

Hajime and his cousins are all working hard to prepare for their examinations, which gives me an opportunity to reply to your letter and to thank you for your lovely New Year's gifts. Tamiko-san's son Ken was very flattered to receive James-san's book (I'm sure he must have written to thank you) and was able to read some of it. He had never received a book autographed by the author. I'm afraid my own English is so poor that I could only make out a few words here and there. I liked the pictures.

Our New Year holidays were pleasant, and Toshiro-san got a slightly higher bonus. He thinks it had something to do with his division getting the Deming Prize. My Noevir wholesaler gave a party for all the Noevir distributors and Noevir Ladies in this district, and there was a party at the community center, where the Association of the Elderly showed the children how to make traditional toys. You remember the bean bags we used to make. Hajime learned how to make those and juggle them. He also learned to make a *takeuma* [literally "bamboo horse"; actually, stilts] and a *take-tonbo* [bamboo dragon fly, made from a pole with a propellor at one end]. Later, the boys made kites and flew them on the bank of the *Arakawa* [Ara River]. There were many folk celebrations from various parts of the country on television. I had never realized how many different ways people celebrate. Now the holidays seem a very long time ago, and the children are working hard, as I said.

We are lucky that Hajime has such a good teacher. It used to be that teachers took more personal interest in the children.

If a child fell behind, the teacher would take extra time to help him and even come to the house to encourage the parents to help. Also, the teachers used to play with the children after school and even take them bicycling and on picnics. Now the schools are afraid that the school may be responsible in the event of an accident, so the teachers are not permitted to do things like that. Most teachers are too busy anyway with school meetings and what not. They have their own interests to pursue on holidays and weekends, and there are very few who concern themselves with the children. I think that a lot of them are teachers simply because they know a government job is safe when the economy is weak; they don't have the dedication that teachers used to have.

Hajime's teacher is a pleasant young man who is not only smart but has a special interest in painting. He takes extra pains to see that Hajime and the others get good instruction in painting as well as in their studies. Most schools pay no attention to such things because they are so intent on having their students prepare for junior high school so that they can pass the examinations to get into good senior high schools. The newspapers announce how many students from each junior high get into which high school and which high school students get into which college or university, so the schools compete to get as many students as they can into the elite school at the next level. The competition is based entirely on scores in the national achievement tests. A junior high school may not permit a student to take the examination for an elite public high school because it is afraid that the student may fail, and the school doesn't want any failures on its record. If he cannot take the examination, the student has no choice but to apply to a less prestigious public school or attend a private high school. The public high schools used to be much better than the private schools; now the private schools have in many cases hired superior teachers, they have improved their reputations, and some of them are actually better than certain public schools.

You wrote to me about James-san's son Jamie being accepted at Harvard and deciding instead to go to a small college where they do nothing but read the classics. That would be like a boy here being accepted at Todai University and turning it down. It would be unthinkable, and when I mentioned it to Toshiro-san he found it hard to believe. How wonderful for a boy to feel free to make that decision. I don't think it could happen here. Poor Hajime is just finishing the second grade and with *juku* and Saturday morning classes he has so little freedom even now. But if he is to have any future, that is what he must accept.

It will not be too many years before I will be worrying about Hajime getting into a good senior high school and then a good university. I probably shouldn't tell you, but Mariko-san's son Ken-ichi had a very difficult time a few years ago. He failed his examination and went to a *yobiko* [*yobi* means preparation; a *yobiko* is a special "cram" school for students preparing for university examinations]. He wants to be a dentist, and this was a special *yobiko* for students who wanted to get into dental school. The people who ran the school told Ken-ichi and Mariko-san that he was not likely to pass the examination, and they tried to persuade Mariko-san to go the *uraguchi nyugaku* route [getting in through the back door], which would have meant putting up a lot of money, most of which would go to bribe the right people to obtain entrance for Ken-ichi. Mariko-san was extremely upset, because they don't have all that much money and because she hated the whole idea. Happily, Ken-ichi did pass the examination and got into dental school without any bribery, but I know that other young men — and even some young women — get into schools on the basis of something other than merit. So many young *ronin* (53) are memorizing English words and mathematical formulas and so forth, which they will forget as soon as the exams are over, that I wonder whether our educational system makes any sense. I know it's wrong for students who cannot pass examinations to be able to have their parents get them into schools through bribery, yet it's also wrong, I think, to place such a high premium on being able to memorize a lot of information. Someone who has trouble memorizing may actually have a more analytical mind and be more capable in other ways than someone who did well on an exam because he was good at memorizing. Shouldn't schools help people learn to *think* instead of just filling their heads with a lot of information?

My business keeps me so busy nowadays that I have not been able to be as active in the P.T.A. (54) as I used to be when I put out the P.T.A. bulletin. Our bulletin won an award two years ago as the best in Saitama Prefecture, and they have had trouble since I left in finding someone to keep up the standards. Each class has to fill five P.T.A. posts, and they have a hard time getting people to take the jobs. Often they just draw straws. Some parents love to complain, and there are a lot of troublemakers. Not many people want to accept responsibility, so it is difficult to find someone qualified to be the class *iin* [director], the person who serves as the chief liaison between teachers and parents. I don't know about other P.T.A.s, but the head of ours is always a man, yet the meetings are usually during the day when very few men are able to attend. When children have problems at school, the parents often go to the board of education instead of speaking directly to the teacher. Parents don't trust teachers the way they used to, and teachers don't trust parents. If a parent asks a teacher for advice, or complains to the teacher, the teacher may blame the child for complaining and may take revenge on the child. A teacher in one school left in the middle of a P.T.A. meeting because she had to pick up her own child at a nursery. That shocked a lot of mothers. All I could say was that the teacher should have planned her schedule better. Certainly teachers with children should be allowed to continue working, but teachers just don't have the passion to teach that they had when I was in school.

What troubles many parents is the violence that has occurred in some schools. I have a friend with a boy in the ninth grade, the last grade of junior high school. It's evidently a terrible school with real discipline problems. In one classroom, some boys played radios at such high volume that nobody could hear the teacher, and the teacher could not stop them. There was a parents meeting every month, and the parents confessed that they could not control their boys. Some parents said they were afraid of their children. You know how big the children have grown since the war (55). Well, in some families, the boys refuse to eat their mothers' food and go out to eat at fast-food places. You saw all the McDonald's and Kentucky Fried Chicken and Mr. Donut places we have now. They stay out long after midnight, and the parents are afraid to say a word. If it came to a physical fight, the father would be no match for the son, so many fathers simply avoid confrontations with their sons. Hajime is big for his age and may grow to be quite tall, but I'm happy to say that he shows no indication of being disobedient. He listens to what we say and he obeys us very well. Toshiro-san says that parents are only human and should not pretend to be perfect. I don't know. Sometimes I think I have two boys instead of one, but I think it has been helpful for Toshiro-san to spend more time with Hajime. In fact, Toshiro-san is quite unlike most Japanese husbands in many ways. For one thing, he sometimes praises me in front of other people, which is really almost unheard of. I know James-san praises you, but did you ever hear *Oto-o-san* say anything nice about *Oka-a-san* in public?

That school with the discipline problems nearly had to cancel its *shugakuryoko* [an excursion for students organized by the school]. I remember how much I looked forward to our *shugakuryoko*, and how we saved up for it for so long. Many of the children at this problem school felt bitterly disappointed, and some parents pleaded to have the school proceed with the *shugakuryoko*. For some of the children, it might be the only time in their lives that they would get to see Nara and Kyoto, so the school agreed. On the morning the group was to leave, the parents came to the school and checked every child's luggage. If anything was found that could cause a disturbance, the child with that item was not permitted to go on the trip, or so I was told. And some parents went along on the trip to make sure that nothing unpleasant happened. As far as I'm concerned, it was unpleasant enough that such measures should have been thought necessary.

The teachers union in Tokyo has established an emergency telephone with two numbers that parents and teachers can call for advice about student violence. Principals and teachers take turns on the phones Mondays, Wednesdays, Fridays, and Saturday afternoons from two to five. All the prefectures outside Tokyo have been expanding so quickly that there is great pressure on the school systems. Most of the school budget goes to expanding classrooms and putting up new buildings, so there is not much left for books, paper, science laboratory equipment, and athletic equipment. The secretary-treasurer of the P.T.A. has to find ways to raise money. At the annual bazaar this year, we raised nearly eight hundred thousand yen [about four thousand dollars], but it's never enough.

Sachiko

Dear Chie,

I finally got to see that interview with Nancy Reagan in *Shufunotomo* — the one everybody made such a fuss about because the magazine paid someone to set up the interview. Fuyuko Kamisaka, who conducted the interview, is quite a popular writer, but I don't think she did a very good job. I mean, she asked dumb questions like, "What do you do to watch over your husband's health?" and "What kind of man is the President?" and "What do you think of feminist criticism of your views?" Kamisaka-san made Mrs. Reagan sound like a typical Japanese wife — obedient and charming — but said she was slightly "mysterious." She wrote that in response to the question about what she did for her husband's health, Mrs. Reagan just "lowered her head in thought" until her aide advised her to say that she recommended reasonable exercise for the President. And when she was asked what kind of man the President was, she "stared into space, looking for the proper words." When she found the words, they were not very original. She said that despite the fact that Ronald Reagan had become a more prominent public figure since entering the White House, "to me, my husband is still my husband... I could not imagine life without (him)."

You wrote that a lot of your women friends were upset about Mrs. Reagan's opposition to abortion and the Equal Rights Amendment. She looks like a nice enough woman — the *Shufunotomo* article goes on for seven pages, with only two pages devoted to the actual interview, and more than half the space is devoted to photographs — but what she said in response to Kamisaka-san's questions made me wonder what goes on in her head. I mean, she defended her stand on abortion by saying that she had had two miscarriages, that she wished her husband could have been in the delivery room during the birth of their children, and that she had received help in strengthening her views on the issue, whatever that means. She also said, "I sometimes say that seventy-five percent of marriage consists of patience and effort. Love is to give and take unstintingly... I feel sorry for those who talk about spontaneity and independence, but who ignore patience and effort."

It's all so obvious. Of course we all have to be patient and put forth some effort, but we don't need Mrs. Reagan to tell us that. I was struck, by the way, with how much effort you make to provide dinner for your stepchildren. It's really quite sweet, and so un-Japanese for a man and his wife to have dinner every week with the man's children by an earlier marriage. Maybe some divorced Japanese men see their children on that basis, but I have not yet heard of it. James-san is divorced, you tell me that one of his sisters is divorced, and you say that many of James-san's friends have been divorced. Our divorce rate has increased a lot, so I'm sure that many divorced people are following Western ways, but I think the American divorce rate is still about eighteen times as high as ours, partly, I suppose, because it is so difficult for a divorced woman in Japan to find employment in a job that will pay her well enough to raise her children.

Your report about the television version of *Shogun* last fall with most of the dialogue in Japanese and no subtitles was amusing. We saw a shorter version that was shown in movie theaters. I agree that the novelist was preposterous when he included that "Lady Mariko" character. It would have been unthinkable for a married woman in the sixteenth century to travel about the country as an interpreter, leaving her *samurai* husband behind. Lady Mariko confesses to Captain Blackthorne in the movie that her family had an ignoble past, and there evidently was an actual woman who vaguely resembles her. You may remember that General Mitsuhide Akechi set

fire to a monastery where the Taira strongman Oda Nobunaga was spending the night in June 1582, and that Nobunaga,
who was trying to unify Japan under one rule, either perished
in the flames or commited *seppuku*. Well, General Akechi had
a daughter Hosokawa who was converted by a Spanish or
Portuguese missionary and took the name Hosokawa Gracia.
She may have been the woman that the novelist had in mind,
but she could hardly have done what Lady Mariko did in the
movie.

Captain Blackthorne, of course, was William Adams, the
man they called Anjin-san [Mr. Engineer]. Did you know that
they still hold a memorial service on April fourteenth every
year at Hirado in Nagasaki? That is where he died in 1620 and
was buried. As for the episode in which one of Blackthorne's
men is tortured in a pot of boiling water, Hajime was fascinated when I told him about the famous thief and murderer
Goemon Ishikawa who wrote the famous poem (I wish I could
find a copy of it). We have a friend with one of those bathtubs
they call a *Goemon Buro*, and you should have seen Hajime's
face when I told him that it was because Goemon Ishikawa
was captured by the soldiers of Hideyoshi Toyotomi toward
the end of the sixteenth century and that he was thrown into a
cauldron of boiling oil.

We had our usual spring transportation strikes here and
the usual token wage increases. It happens every year, so
nobody was too upset. Toshiro-san's company had booked
some hotel rooms so he didn't come home for two nights, that
was all. Nothing like the big strike you wrote about in New
York last year.

Sachiko

12 *April*

Dear Chie,

Today was the last Sunday for *hanami* [cherry blossom viewing], at least in this part of the country. The *sakura* [cherry blossoms] are beginning to fall quickly, and I'm happy that we had such a nice day for the people who had not yet seen them.

With the weather getting warm again, I am more aware of the street noises. You remember the loudspeakers on the trucks blaring *"ishi yaki imo"* [sweet potatoes baked on hot stones] and all the other things they sell. Is it the same in New York? The *chirigami kokan* [toilet paper exchanger] (57) just went by with his truck. We don't give our wastepaper to him anymore because our P.T.A. has a contract with a collector who sends us a receipt which we turn over to the P.T.A. The collector picks up our paper and empty bottles twice a month, he redeems the receipts from the P.T.A., and that is how we finance our P.T.A. activities. We have to buy our toilet paper at the store instead of getting it from the *chirigami kokan* the way we used to, but it's a nice way to raise money for the P.T.A., and the paper gets recycled just as it would the old way.

The reason I'm going on about this is that somebody just told me Kazuko Fukuda's husband was a *chirigami kokan*. You may remember my writing to you about Fukuda-san, the one who played *pachinko* and tried to sell me life insurance. She is now one of my Noevir Ladies, and she is doing quite well, but now I understand why I felt there was something mysterious about her. She was simply embarrassed, I think, and didn't want anybody to know why she had divorced her husband. I know I shouldn't listen to gossip, especially about my Noevir Ladies, but I was interested and I thought you might be, so I'm writing to you instead of spreading stories where they might hurt someone.

There really isn't anything disreputable about being a *chirigami kokan*, and Fukuda-san should be proud that her husband had the courage to become one, I think. After all, it wasn't his fault that his business went bankrupt. That's the risk you take when you have your own business, and Fukuda-san's husband wasn't the first person to have his business fold and to prefer working for himself than taking orders from someone else. I like the idea of being my own boss, too, so I know exactly how he must have felt. In fact, I understand that some *chirigami kokan* are men with prestigious university degrees who either failed in business or who just do not like the discipline required when you work for a big company. It pains me to think of Fukuda-san living her lonely life — a divorced woman here is still a *demodori* [girl who has "gone out and come back"] with little chance of remarriage — and I suspect that her ex-husband is lonely, too, especially since most people think of what he does as being somehow contemptible. If only I could think of something to say to her that would help her to see him in a different light.

Maybe I could say something positive about re-cycling. One of Noevir's slogans, and it's in English, is "Only One World." I like that. There is something wholesome about it. When I think of all the trees that are cut down to produce newsprint I have to wonder what we are doing with the earth's resources. Granted, trees are a renewable resource, but if we cut down more than we grow we will be in trouble. It's much better to use recycled paper and bottles, and the government's Paper Recycling Promotion Center should do something to make people realize what an important job the *chirigami kokan* are doing.

You asked about the air pollution. It is a problem, but I think it's getting better. A lot of things are improving. The city now provides free water-resistant paper bags for garbage. The bags are not plastic because the garbage is burned, and burning plastic creates more pollutants. If we run out of bags, we have to buy extras, but we generally get by on what the city hands out. Garbage from about twenty families is placed in one spot and is picked up twice a week. Glass bottles and jars, magazines, and newspapers are all recycled.

Changing the subject, I was fascinated to hear from you that our grandmother had shaved eyebrows and black false teeth. Of course I never knew her and I had no idea that women still stained their teeth as recently as that. I read somewhere that the royal family adopted the practice of *ohaguro* [staining teeth black] in the year 1233 as a sign of beauty for both men and women, and that married women had to shave their eyebrows and blacken their teeth until 1876, when the Meiji empress stopped doing it. It said that men used to whiten their faces, too, and not just for the Kabuki Theater. Somewhere else I read that before the Meiji Restoration men wore their hair long in a variety of different styles but always with a topknot. In fact, one punishment for a *samurai* was to order him to have his hair cut. A *samurai* accused of some offense by his master might cut his hair to prove his loyalty. After the Meiji Restoration, men cut their hair and some women did, too, because long hair was uncomfortable and not very practical. The government did not like the idea of women cutting their hair, and in 1872 they passed a law imposing a fine on any woman who cut her hair. I remember when you wore your hair down to your waist; so did Yoko-san and I. Now I think Mariko-san back in Yonago is the only one of us who still has long hair.

Women's Week began here Friday, and it was the thirty-fifth anniversary of women having the vote and electing thirty-four women to the Diet. I never realized before that it was the government that organized Women's Week — specifically the Department of Women and Juveniles in the Ministry of Labor. Now we have only twenty-three women in the Diet, and I think I wrote to you after the election last year what kind of women they tend to elect. Even though more of us go to the polls than men, women are too apathetic, I'm afraid.

Women here still make most of the buying decisions. When a merchant wants to sell men's overcoats or hats, he directs his advertising to women, because women have the money and decide what to buy. The head of Onward, the big men's clothing maker, has said that seventy percent of the men bring their wives with them when they buy clothes, which is why we have advertising for men's clothing in women's magazines. There was an article about that somewhere. I saved it so that I could send it to you, and now I can't find it. Anyway, it said that Japanese and West Germans spend more money for clothing than people anywhere else in the world — an average of one hundred thousand yen [about five hundred dollars] per person each year. Sales of men's and children's clothing have been decreasing, though, while sales of women's clothing have been increasing. That's because more women are working and making more money and because not so many of us are making our own clothes anymore.

Those Vogue patterns you sent me were wonderful — we have nothing like that here — and I wish I still had time for dressmaking. Now the business takes up too much of my attention and some lovely fabric that I bought is still sitting in the closet.

If only women would put some of their energies to work on our political and social problems. Medical education is a good example. Every year we seem to have a scandal connected with a professor selling examination papers or accepting a payoff to admit a student who could not pass the entrance examination to medical school or dental school. It is an open secret that even the best medical schools require a huge donation from applicants in addition to the tuition. I don't know how much it costs now, but a few years ago someone published figures showing that Kanazawa Medical School demanded a donation of ¥ 15,300,000 [about $76,500], Osaka Medical School demanded ¥ 11,300,000 [about $56,500], Tokyo Women's Medical School got eleven million yen [about fifty-five thousand dollars], Juntendo University Medical School required ¥ 10,500,000 [about $52,500], and Kurume University Medical School got ¥ 9,500,000 [about $47,500]. Obviously, only someone with rich parents can get into medical school, and some people say that they cannot have much confidence in Japanese doctors when they know that entrance to medical school is based on something other than ability. Is it that way in America?

You wrote that there were not many women physicians in America, and of course that is true in Japan as well. I did read about the first Japanese woman to receive a license to practice medicine when the first government examinations were given in March 1885. Her name was Ginko Hagino, and she was thirty-four at the time. She had been married at sixteen, had contracted a sexually transmitted disease from her husband, who then divorced her, and had received treatment from male physicians. She felt that there should be women gynecologists, so she studied and got her license. The first woman to enter a medical school was Mitsuko Takahashi, who was thirty-three when she entered Saisei Gakusha in 1884. She got her license three years later. Younger women evidently began studying medicine then, and Yae Yoshioka was only twenty-two when she got out of Saisei Gakusha and obtained her license in 1889. Saisei Gakusha was the only private medical school then, and it was difficult to have female students because there was so much public opposition to mixing the sexes in those days. A woman physician named Yae Yoshioka was working at Shisei Hospital in 1900 and started Tokyo Girls' Medical School at that time in one room of the hospital. The first school to train women nurses was established in 1905 at *Seiroka byoin* [St. Luke's Hospital].

That is all I was able to find out. I think women should work to get more government support for the medical schools rather than the schools being forced to demand donations. And I agree that there should be more women physicians. It's one more example of women's ability being wasted. We celebrate Women's Week, yet not many of us think about the terrible waste of womanpower in the world. They say that the number of part-time women workers jumped twenty-five percent between 1976 and 1980, but the total was still only 2.6 million, and too many people still believe that having married women work is a threat to family stability.

A lot of young women go to college nowadays, and I mean four-year colleges. The number of women graduates this year was ninety-six thousand, nearly twice what it was ten years ago, but the women have trouble finding jobs. A man at the university may receive a stack of recruitment literature one meter high, while a woman, even if she is a law student, receives nothing except, maybe, a list of questions such as, "Do you plan to work all your life or will you quit when you get married?" and "Do you have enough self-confidence to continue working after you have a child?" I heard about a girl whose first name could have been a boy's name. She received a lot of recruitment literature, but when she applied for a job the company wrote back that it did not hire four-year college graduates if they were women and wished her good luck. Men who have spent most of their time in college playing *mahjong* get good job offers while women who did well get passed over. The Equal Rights Amendment prohibits discrimination on the basis of sex with regard to civil service jobs, but private industry is not required to treat women like men when there are jobs to be filled.

Fujitsu, the big computer maker, has been sending re-cruiters to women's colleges because of a shortage in male software engineers. They hired twenty-five female software engineers in 1979. The women make as much as the men, and

Fujitsu expects to have one hundred and fifty by the spring of 1982. Of course that's high technology and it's a special case.

A woman closer to my own field is Kazuko Ishihara, who became the first woman executive at Takashimaya [the large department store chain] in 1979. She was a graduate of a well-known four-year women's college, yet it took her twenty-seven years to reach the executive level. She had to begin as a shoe clerk and do that for five years while she watched men who had been hired at the same time get promoted to higher positions. She also worked in the housewares department and in infants wear. And after having two babies herself she suggested a couple of items that became big hits at Takashimaya. One was a practical, yet fashionable, maternity dress, and the other was a ventilated diaper cover. She was interviewed by someone from the *Mainichi Shimbun* and I got a copy of the story to read to my Noevir Ladies.

What Ishihara-san said, and I think my Noevir Ladies should know it, was this: "Working is not easy. If you stay home you don't have the humiliations you experience when you work. Work is a continuing series of humiliations, and you must accept merciless reproaches, differing opinions, and criticisms to the point where it wears you out. If you work, you must examine the purpose of your life and ask yourself why you are working. Unless you know the answer very clearly, you cannot continue."

Needless to say, I think I am quite clear about why I want to work, and so far it has not been the humiliating experience Ishihara-san says it is.

Sachiko

10 *May*

Dear Chie,

Monday was a holiday (Constitution Day was Sunday), Tuesday was *Tango-no-sekku* [Boys' Day Festival], as well as *Kodomo-no-hi* [Children's Day], so we had a short week. Toshiro-san helped Hajime hang his paper *koinobori* [carp banner] out the window (57), and we put out the *kabuto* [miniature samurai helmet] and *nobori* [miniature samurai banner] that Hajime received from Toshiro-san's parents on his first *Tango-no-sekku*. On the TV news they showed a farmhouse in the country with a huge pole from which every son in the house had his *koinobori* blowing in the wind. Hajime was satisfied with his little one.

Yesterday was his birthday (58) and I bought steak, which he adores. It is terribly expensive, as you know — two thousand yen for two hundred grams [roughly twenty dollars per pound] if you want anything decent, so I only got a little; it was Kobe beef and not the best Matsuzaka beef, which can cost twice as much. I remember when James-san came over here with steak from your butcher and had it impounded at Narita Airport (59). We did not know whether to laugh or cry.

The holiday gave me a chance to catch up on some paperwork. I won't bore you with the details, but my business has grown very quickly. Some of my Noevir Ladies are fantastic. I find that they fall roughly into two groups, and this may interest you. The ones who do well never complain. The others are always telling me about their problems, and when they are unsuccessful they use their husbands as an excuse. They say, "*Watashino shujin...*" ["My master..."]. Those women don't do too well. As for the others, if one of them has sales of at least one million yen [about five thousand dollars] per month for three months in a row, the company invites her

∽ 99

on an overseas holiday, generally to Guam, for one week. I have to complete my inventory report by the twentieth of each month and I turn my revenues over to my wholesaler at the end of the month. The revenues have really been climbing. I work very hard, but I love it. I only wish that I had more time to get out into the country in this lovely weather.

Okura-san, the head of Noevir, likes the outdoor life more than anything else, and he sometimes takes people in the company hiking, fishing, sailing, and skiing. Those who cannot ski are given instruction in the mountains at Happo-on-e. He especially likes fishing in the mountain streams for iwana [a large land-locked fish of the salmon family]. It reaches eighty centimeters in length and has been known to eat small animals that come to drink at the stream. Okura-san says it is a good fighting fish. He believes that sport is good for returning humans to contact with their animal instincts and helping them to regain the vitality that people had in ages past.

Some of Okura-san's ideas are a little macho for me. ("Macho" is the word you use, isn't it?) For one thing, he has this approach book and an eighty-second talk for Noevir Ladies to give potential customers. It may be very effective for some women, but I wonder about the example he uses when he explains it. During the Pacific War, he says, the Mitsubishi Sentoki [Zero] fighter plane was difficult to fly and required experienced pilots. We lost so many pilots that we had to train new ones very quickly, and you just could not learn to fly that plane very quickly. It did not take more than three to six months to learn to fly a Grumman or Lockheed fighter plane, but it took much longer — much too long — to learn to fly the Mitsubishi Sentoki. Okura-san says that if he had to depend on top-flight sales people, he would have to spend a lot of time on training and education, but with his eighty-second talk and his approach book, anybody can be a good sales person.

He also likes to quote Konosuke Matsushita, the head of National Panasonic, whose business philosophy is that he makes merchandise involving electricity (60) but what he is really doing is improving the lives of the people who work for him and only incidentally producing merchandise. According to Matsushita, people say about business that sometimes you make money and sometimes you lose money, but business is really like two *samurai* fighting with swords. The loser dies. In business you must succeed or you are dead. Every business must have men of talent and big capital. To use those talents and that capital and not succeed is a crime. Business must make a contribution to the public, and the bigger the contribution it makes the higher its reward will be. I like that except for the part about *samurai* fighting to the death and the fact that it's all so male-oriented.

In fairness to Matsushita-san, who is now in his eighties, he chose a young man to be president of the company in 1977. The man was twenty-fifth from the top, so a lot of higher-ups must have been upset, but Matsushita said the world was changing and the company needed people with fresh ideas for an international management system. And in fairness to Okura-san, he does hire men and women on an equal basis and he speaks out against *dansonjohi* [male supremacy]. Women in Japan today have educations comparable to those of men, they have fewer children, and since women are able to bear children they have a lot of strength, he says, and that strength is being wasted. It almost sounds like what I have been saying, doesn't it? He also has a lot of respect for women, he says, because a woman saved him from bankruptcy. (You may remember my writing to you about the wife of his friend who showed him that his Rubbermaid dishracks could be sold by the same method as Tupperware; that's who he has in mind when he talks about a woman saving him from bankruptcy, and I guess she did.)

There are now women in air control towers at airports, and there are even one hundred and fifty commercial pilots who are women, according to Okura-san. That's not many out of the forty thousand commercial pilots in the world, but it's a beginning. Okura-san just got a Cessna 120 jet that he says he will use to visit sub-branches and wholesalers. By the way, I hear that in October they are going to open a sub-branch right here in Omiya City. Okura-san had been using his smaller Cessna propellor plane to visit the sub-branches at least once a month. Now he's letting one of his pilots take employees to resorts in that plane on weekends.

Commercial tour operators here are less idealistic than Okura-san. As you may have heard, some of them offer tours that take men to places such as Taiwan, the Philippines, Thailand, and — most especially — South Korea for no other purpose than to have sex with young prostitutes. It's disgusting, and I think Japan is the only country with tours of that sort (61). I can't understand how any woman could let her husband take such a tour. Most of the men who go are in their fifties and sixties, men who don't know how to relate to women, including their own wives, because our education and our society give boys no preparation for normal man-woman relationships. So many women's magazines have stories about consciousness-raising, but nothing is done to raise the consciousness of men, and that is the problem. The magazines say we must raise boys differently, and that women must speak up for what they want, but young men continue to behave the way they always have done. It is hard to change the way your father behaves, or your brother, or your husband, or even your son, and I cannot see that the situation is improving. It may even be getting worse.

I read in one magazine that until 1960 both boys and girls had to take home economics through high school, and that boys in elementary school learned sewing and embroidery. Now boys take technical training in junior high and only the girls continue with home economics. Tamiko-san's boy Tadashi did a lovely piece of embroidery in the sixth grade. It was pretty enough to frame and hang on the wall. What a pity that the system discourages him from continuing. All the pictures of women in Hajime's social studies book show them in the kitchen or taking care of babies, and all the professionals shown are men. The book says that a woman's job is to serve the family. It says nothing about women having opportunities outside the home, or about equal rights and equal pay for women as spelled out in the 1947 law. Tamiko-san showed me a high school home economics book with a chapter entitled "Marriage to Old Age." The father in the "typical" family the book portrayed had a position as a *sarariman* [salaried man] with a company, the wife worked with him until she had her first child, and she retired after the baby was born. Tamiko-san tells me that in the older textbooks the wife retired at marriage. The second child comes when the first one is three or four years old in the new book, and when the second child enters elementary school, the mother gets some kind of job. Without any explanation, the book shows the mother retiring when she is forty-seven, and when she is fifty she has her first grandchild. The husband retires when he is sixty and gets another job. This is the family pattern handed down to schoolgirls. They are told that they must plan for a future roughly along the lines in the textbook.

Somebody interviewed Okura-san, the president of Noevir, about Japanese society, and he insisted that it was going to change. He said that men have been able to dominate our society because it is basic to men's nature to group together. They don't mind wearing uniforms and they can be organized more easily than women, who prefer to be more distinctive in appearance and are more individualistic. He says that individual ability is going to count for more than group harmony in the future, and that men will no longer be so dominant. Most companies give men motivation to succeed and ignore the women, Okura-san told the interviewer, whereas he is good at motivating women. He's certainly right when he says that many young women with talent and ability give up after working for a while in a big company because they see no future for themselves with the company. I'm happier every day that I chose a different course. I just wish they would do something about the educational system to help people grow up with different attitudes regarding men's roles and women's roles.

Sachiko

4 *July*

Dear Chie,

It's very warm here today, and Toshiro-san is watching Hajime play baseball. I just finished clearing up some paperwork connected with my business and thought I would write an answer to your nice letter.

You asked about Noevir and how well it was doing in relation to other cosmetics companies. Well, I just learned recently that as of April the company had four hundred thousand Noevir Ladies and Noevir Maids (That's what we call users) and that sales were at the rate of fifty billion yen [about two hundred and fifty million dollars] per year. At the end of 1978, there were only four thousand Noevir Ladies, so you can see that the company has grown very quickly — quite amazing when you realize how many dozens of companies are trying to sell cosmetics on a door-to-door basis. The leading brand sold door-to-door is still Pola, with Menard number two. In 1979, a company called Oppen was third, Avon was fourth, Yakuruto [originally a yogurt producer] fifth, Norris sixth, Yamano seventh, Flouveil (Okura-san's old company) eighth, Chanson ninth, and Seabon tenth. Noevir has now passed all except the top two and has started to build a big new factory outside Yokaichi City, near Lake Biwa in Shiga Prefecture.

My own business is doing so well that I have finally bought a car. It's a two-door Mazda, light tan. I got it second-hand and Hajime just loves it. Toshiro-san is a little dubious because, as he says, the roads are so crowded that it's usually faster to take the train (62). That's true on weekends and holidays, but sometimes it is impossible to get on a train or to get to certain places except by car. Gasoline now costs one hundred and sixty yen per liter [more than three dollars per gallon]; three years ago it was only about one hundred yen per liter [just under two dollars per gallon], so driving is definitely an extravagance. I read somewhere that we pay about twice as much per liter as Americans do, but I guess the distances here are much shorter. I was interested to read in your letter that so many Americans buy cars on the installment plan. In our case, I had enough money from the business to pay cash. That is what most people do, I think. Don't the Americans pay an awful lot in interest on their car loans?

Here, depending on what kind of car you have, it costs fifty to sixty thousand yen [two hundred and fifty to three hundred dollars] every other year for taxes and insurance on the car, and the government requires car-owners to have their vehicles inspected every two years. That generally costs another fifty thousand yen at a licensed repair shop, but if the car is big or needs a lot of work you pay more. Toshiro-san insists that we must have the car inspected every six months, which is not required but is probably a good idea. They change the oil, install anti-freeze in the fall, and check the main elements, such as the brakes. If you have an accident, the six-month inspection certificate shows that you were not negligent in keeping your car safe. I've learned how to drive quite well and I don't intend to have any accidents, but I guess Toshiro-san is right. I don't know how many cars and trucks are now on the road. I did see somewhere that we now have more than forty million licensed drivers. A lot of those — more than one third — are women drivers like me. Whether they are all as careful as I am is another story. The government has checkpoints to test the breath of drivers for alcohol, and there are services to provide drivers for people who have had too much to drink, but there is still a lot of drunken driving.

We could have bought a brand-new car, but we are saving our money to buy a house (63). Yes, a house of our own. Two years ago that, like the car, was only a dream, but our fortunes have improved thanks to my increased income. While we don't want to jeopardize Hajime's education money, we think we can manage it, even though housing prices have gone up a lot, because Toshiro-san's company will help us finance it and I hope to be able to contribute a good deal. When Yoko-san bought her house at the end of 1972, she paid only ¥ 11,618,263 [about fifty-nine thousand dollars], including the property. Tax included, she put down five million yen [about twenty-five thousand dollars] and borrowed the rest from *Dai-Ichi Seimei Hoken Gaisha* [Number One Life Insurance Company]. The loan is spread out over eighteen years and is divided into two parts. Yoko-san pays thirty-three thousand yen [about one hundred and sixty-five dollars] each month, and she pays two hundred and twenty-thousand yen [about eleven hundred dollars] once a year when Teruo-san receives his yearend bonus. The *Jutaku kinyu koko* [Housing Finance Corporation] loans money at only 5.6 percent, but that is subsidized by the government and is only available for houses that cost five or six million yen [twenty-five to thirty thousand dollars], so Yoko-san's interest began at eight percent and has gone up to nine percent because of the inflation. In our case, Toshiro-san's company will loan us money against his retirement pay and we will not have to pay such a high rate of interest.

You wrote that the enormous interest rates in America had discouraged people from buying houses because they could not afford to take out mortgages at eighteen or twenty percent interest. Here the interest rates are about eight-and-a-half percent, and some companies arrange it so that their employees hardly have to pay any interest at all. The problem isn't high interest. The problem is that construction costs have gone way up and what they call "real income" is down because people have to pay more for so many things. So while many of us complain about lack of space, lack of sunlight, and lack of greenery, Tokyo has twenty-thousand new *manshons* [condominium apartments, euphemestically called "mansions"] that remain vacant because nobody can afford to buy them.

You described the Japanese-style house that James-san's younger sister has in East Hampton, and it sounds fantastic. I'm sure that a house with so much property here, even one that far out of the city, would cost well over two hundred million yen [about one million dollars]. The construction industry here is worse than it has been in nearly fifteen years. A lot of people say that the government has pumped the nation's wealth into expanding and upgrading industry at the expense of housing, with the result that too many people have to live in what we call *usagigoya* [rabbit hutches]. Prices have gone up so much since Yoko-san bought her house that the same two-story house, including the property, now costs ¥ 43,158,000 [about two hundred and sixteen thousand dollars]. That house has fifty-six *tsubo* [about one hundred and eighty-five square meters, or about two thousand square feet] and three bedrooms, which is more than we need, so perhaps we won't have to pay that much. Still, it will not be cheap. Most people here pay fifty or sixty thousand yen [two hundred and fifty to three hundred dollars] per month because they cannot afford down payments as high as Yoko-san made. Some people even pay one hundred thousand yen [about five hundred dollars], not counting what they pay out of the yearend bonus.

Apartment rents are still fairly low. The closer you get to the railroad station, the higher the rent. Many people ride their bicycles to the station, and it has got to the point where there is hardly any place to leave your bike. You wrote that people in New York often remove the front wheels of their bikes when they leave them on the street to discourage anyone from stealing them. Here the problem is not theft but rather what we call *jitensha kogai* [bicycle pollution]. There are just too many bicycles for the available space (64).

We are not too close to the station, as you know, so for what they call a 2DK [two rooms with dining kitchen, bathroom, and toilet], we pay fifty thousand yen [two hundred and fifty dollars] per month. Many people with apartments this small have two and even three children, so relatively speaking we are not too crowded, and we have been able to save quite a lot by having a low rent. One reason I have been reluctant to buy a house, even though I could see the prices going up, was that so many people here had to give up their houses because of business reverses. If a man works for a big company and the company does not pay its usual yearend bonus, he may have to borrow from a *sarakin* [short for *sarariman kinyu*, or salaried man's loan company]. Some of them are as large as regular banks, and the interest rates they charge are outrageous — ten percent per month, or one hundred and twenty percent per year. And if you miss a monthly payment you have to pay another two percent interest. One month's interest is deducted in advance, and there is no law against charging that rate of interest so long as it is no higher.

I was visiting Yoko-san one evening a few weeks ago and I was shocked to hear some men shouting outside another house in the neighborhood. Yoko-san explained that the man who lived in that house worked for a company which had failed to pay bonuses last December, so he had had to borrow from a *sarakin* to make his yearend mortgage loan payment. A *sarakin* is often controlled by *yakuza* [gamblers or gangsters], and when someone falls behind in his payments, the sarakin sends out collectors. They often look like *yakuza* themselves, and they come at all hours of the day or night — even after midnight. They shout out the names of the people who owe them money, and although the lights may be out in the house because the people are pretending to be away, the collectors call out, "We know you're in there. Why don't you come out and pay us? We want our money." Yoko-san told me that the people were afraid to make a sound, and that it was especially horrible because the family had a boy about Hajime's age. Everyone in the neighborhood could hear what was going on, and aside from everything else it was embarrassing. There are always stories in the newspaper about such incidents, and I know of two families that had to move out and let the *sarakin* take over their houses. Yoko-san knows some others, and I'm sure it has happened to many families with whom I am not familiar. Toshiro-san and I don't want to get ourselves into an uncomfortable situation financially, so we have been very cautious.

When I was growing up in Yonago, I often got upset because so many women used to come to our mother asking for advice. Sometimes there were visitors from morning until night. Now I find that my Noevir Ladies come to me for advice. I try to keep the conversation directed to business, but you know how it is. Often they tell me about problems they are having in their families. The mother-in-law of one Noevir Lady is actually the husband's stepmother. Her real son was taken away from her when her first husband died. It was during the war, and the husband's family took the boy to make sure that the family property would not have to be divided with the widow. The boy couldn't have been much older than Hajime is now when he was taken from her, and when I think about that poor woman being deprived of her son it makes me terribly sad and angry. Just suppose someone took Hajime away from me without my having any way to prevent it. I had to weep when the woman told me the story, and it made me realize how close we still are to the old days when women had no rights at all.

Other Noevir Ladies tell me about troubles they are having in their marriages, and I find that thinking about their problems helps me find solutions to my own. You know how difficult it is for women to talk about sex, but some of my Noevir Ladies have gradually become more open about discussing such things. I am hardly an authority on sex. The women's magazines here have become quite frank in their articles about sex, but I have trouble relating my own feelings to what I read in the magazine articles. Women used to be brought up to believe that they were not supposed to express their emotions, that their chief function was to bear children rather than to fulfill their own needs. We are not taught that anymore, but it is still part of our character, so when we have problems, we still find it difficult to talk about them openly with anyone. I shouldn't take the time to discuss personal matters with my Noevir Ladies, but I feel that even if I cannot offer any advice I should at least listen. They are so grateful to have someone listen and sympathize.

Sachiko

11 *July*

Dear Chie,

Tuesday was *Tanabata Matsuri* (65), and the hottest day so far this year. Although we prayed for a clear evening, we were disappointed. Hajime stayed up long past his bedtime hoping to see the stars in the Milky Way, but finally he could not keep his eyes open any longer. His calligraphy has improved tremendously (66), and I think he believes that the stars may have had something to do with that. I know I did, and I remember how kind and encouraging you were to me when I was that age. School will soon be over, and Hajime is looking forward to his vacation. We have found a resort on the Izu Peninsula near Shimoda and plan to drive down together with Toshiro-san in the Mazda for a few days. I think it will be educational for Hajime to visit Shimoda.

One of Hajime's best friends from *juku* is a little farm boy. This used to be a big farming area, you know, and although the farmers seemed hostile in the beginning and shut out the city people who moved into the houses and apartments that went up here, they are beginning to mix with us newcomers little by little, and they are very kind when you get to know them. Some of the families have been here for centuries, and now their children go to the same junior high school as the city people. There are even a few among the eleven to twelve hundred pupils in Hajime's elementary school, although his friend from *juku* is not one of them. Goodness knows what the farm children will do when they grow up. The government pays the farmers not to grow rice, so although some of them produce very good vegetables there are so many idle fields full of weeds that farming does not appear to have a bright future in these parts.

Although it is very warm today, the winter was so cold and snowy that it hurt poultry farmers. Hens laid fewer eggs, so fewer chickens were produced. Now the price of chicken is higher, and they're talking about importing more frozen chicken legs from the United States. I read that we prefer the leg and that Americans prefer the breast, and that this is one reason why the frozen chicken is much cheaper than the fresh chicken we raise here, but I still prefer chicken fresh. You say that chicken is much cheaper than fish or red meat even in America, and I wondered if you bought frozen chicken.

I was interested in your comment on how American wives help their husbands in business by charming the higher-ups at conventions and at cocktail parties. That is so completely alien to our business world, in which wives play no role at all. I wonder if I like the American way. How does anyone ever know whether a friendship is sincere or is just cultivated for business reasons? If someone did give a party like that here, it would probably not be in his own house. Some people do have what they call Western-style houses, and some of them are fairly large, but not many houses have rooms as large as the ones I have seen in American movies, and it would be awkward to have the kind of party that you talk about in a Japanese house. Of course many men here curry favor with other men for business purposes, but no women are involved. Toshiro-san told me about someone he knows who plays golf with his clients. The man makes large bets on the matches, and then deliberately loses. It's his way of ingratiating himself. Toshiro-san also told me something rather interesting about Dentsu, the big advertising agency. Somebody told him that the way Dentsu became so big was through political connections. After the war, when government people who had been in power during the war were having trouble finding jobs, Dentsu made a point of hiring them. Eventually, the men either regained power or had friends who got into high positions, and when television came along (67) they were able to pull strings that permitted Dentsu to lock up the best time periods on commercial television and sell them to Dentsu clients. Is that the way American advertising agencies operate? It all seems rather corrupt. Sometimes I think our whole society is corrupt, but I wonder if other societies are any better. What I like about our festivals, especially *Tanabata Matsuri*, is the quality of innocence they have. I hope we never lose that sense of innocence. And I hope that next year we will have a clear evening for *Tanabata Matsuri*.

I was also interested in what you wrote about the Japanese couple in your building. You say that he is very successful and that the company provides them with a car, and so forth. Toshiro-san says that any Japanese businessman who takes an overseas position is in danger of being labeled a foreign specialist and losing his opportunity to get into the company's top management. He says that the man in your building may enjoy the freedom of being outside Japan and be willing to pay the price because he gets paid more than he would at home, but he would have a much brighter future in the company if he were in the home office. Toshiro-san also says that the man's son will have to grow up in Japan if he ever expects to get anywhere; otherwise he will never be accepted as a Japanese. I'm not sure that Toshiro-san is correct about all this; he sometimes has strong ideas that are not altogether well-founded. What you tell me about the school for Japanese children in New York makes me think that this may be one of those matters on which Toshiro-san is generalizing and ignoring some exceptions. In any event, he says that if his company sent him overseas he would go alone and leave me and Hajime here so that Hajime would not suffer as boys do when they grow up outside Japan. He also says that wives of Japanese businessmen in New York have difficult lives, not only because of language problems and culture shock but because women in the Japanese community there are so status-conscious (68). You would know more about that than I.

Sachiko

6 August

Dear Chie,

This is the thirty-sixth anniversary of the bombing of Hiroshima. It was another working day for me, but I was just watching the evening news on television and saw that many people observed the occasion with demonstrations for peace and a ban on nuclear weapons. The *Gensuibaku Kinshi Taikai* [Conference to Prohibit Nuclear Arms] is going on again in Tokyo and Hiroshima with people from many countries. But now it is very political and has lost the purity of being a simple appeal from mothers the way it was originally. I remember your telling me a few years ago, when we sent that delegation to the demonstration in New York with a petition bearing hundreds of thousands of names, that it attracted almost no attention in the media. Japan, of course, is the only country that ever experienced a nuclear attack. I hope and pray there never will be any more of them anywhere.

There have been stories in the newspapers about demonstrations against nuclear energy facilities, and I can understand how those people feel. On the other hand, I wonder whether we can afford not to use nuclear energy. I don't know what the situation is now, but I have a magazine here that says Japan had to import 99.8 percent of her oil in 1978, whereas the United States had to import only 44.5 percent. We depended on oil for forty-eight percent of our energy needs in 1978, and we still use a lot of oil. Nuclear energy accounted for less than four percent of our energy. The United States was more than seventy-eight percent self-sufficient in terms of energy in 1978, the magazine says, and Japan was less than fourteen percent self-sufficient. So while I am sympathetic to the anxieties of those demonstrators I am also concerned about being too dependent on imported energy.

◇114

I remember that when James-san was here he joked that Japanese houses were so cold in February that it was like camping out at the North Pole. If he were here now, in August, he would be happy that our houses let in so much fresh air. Of course the Americans use a lot more energy per person than we Japanese do. Maybe that's because it gets so cold over there in the winter (I noticed that the Canadians use even more energy per person than the Americans). The magazine article said there was something called the International Energy Agency, which measures average energy consumption per person in terms of what they call "tons oil equivalent." In 1978, the world average was five. Japanese consumption was 3.08, the American average was 8.49, the Canadian average 9.03. We Japanese do use a lot more electricity than we did in our mother's time, with television sets, electric rice cookers, electric blankets, water heaters, and so forth.

I suppose that if they were to put up a nuclear plant in Omiya City I might have some anxieties. When I think about the possibilities of a war in the Middle East or another oil embargo, though, I realize how dangerous it is for us to be so dependent on imported oil. Anyway, those Middle Eastern countries know that their oil is going to run out some day and are investing their trillions of yen in ways they hope will cushion their future, when they no longer have such large incomes from oil. What are we doing to prepare ourselves for that future? I worry about that, and I should think the Americans would be worried, too, since they use so much more energy than we do.

A great deal of my own energy goes into helping my Noevir Ladies increase their business. Some of them are fabulous. They don't really have much trouble finding customers. The products are better and the prices are lower than those of some other cosmetics, such as Pola, although that is still the number one brand sold door-to-door. One of my Noevir

Ladies used to be a saleswoman for another door-to-door cosmetics line. She had to be at the office at nine o'clock every morning, work until three in the afternoon, and make twenty calls each day to get new customers. Earlier, she had worked as an Office Lady for a Toyota subcontractor. Her husband worked for the same company, and when he was promoted to the management level the company thought it was not appropriate for her to continue working as a clerk, so she quit and became a cosmetics saleswoman. She had sales of between four hundred and five hundred thousand yen [two thousand to twenty-five hundred dollars] per month, but she's doing even better as a Noevir Lady. She has switched about half her old customers to Noevir products, and she has obtained a lot of new customers by giving samples to prospects. After a few days, she comes back to pick up the sample and ask the woman how she liked it. It may not be the best technique for everyone, but it works for her.

You asked me how I had been so successful. You must understand that I almost never do any actual cosmetics selling. What I do is recruit women to be Noevir Ladies, and I still use the party technique to do that. When I heard that I would have to get one hundred and fifty women, I did not see how I would ever do it. You may remember that Tamiko-san got me started with a tea party. Now I get one after another of my Noevir Ladies to give parties and invite some of their friends. I talk to the women as one housewife to another, I flatter them a little, I tell them something about Noevir, and quite a few want to become Noevir Ladies. If I cannot persuade them to do that, I often manage to get them to buy some Noevir products and become what we call Noevir Maids, which makes them customers of the woman who gives the party. I now have nearly one hundred and seventy Noevir Ladies. Instead of being a second distributor I am now a first distributor, and I'm thinking of becoming a wholesaler. Some wholesalers have several dozen distributors like me with hundreds and hundreds of Noevir Ladies. Funny, isn't it? I got into this business simply with the idea of making a little extra money. Do I really want to be a big wholesaler? I don't know.

Hajime enjoyed Shimoda very much, as we all did. Thank you for asking. No, of course I did not tell him about the mistress that Taunzento Harisu [Townsend Harris] kept (69). When he saw the place where the first beef had been slaughtered for human consumption in Japan, he was quite excited (I've told you how much he likes steak), and he was also interested to hear that nobody here drank cows' milk until then. The butchers of Tokyo erected the monument commemorating the beef slaughtering just fifty years ago, in 1931, and while that made our visit seem important to Hajime I think he was most impressed by the fact that an American had had so much influence on the Japanese so long ago. He talked all the way home about his *obasan* [aunt] in America, and he laughed when I told him what you wrote about James-san's older boy Oliver liking *sushi*. It has been more than two years since he saw you, and I suspect that his memory of you is based more on the photographs we have than on actual recollection.

Sachiko

Dear Chie,

Everybody here is talking about Chiyo Kuwabara. She's one of the women who has just climbed a five thousand four hundred and twenty-five meter peak in the Himalayas and she's sixty-four. The other woman on the expedition, a physician, is sixty-five, but for some reason Kuwabara-san is getting more attention in the press. Maybe it's because more older women can identify with her. You are older than I so perhaps you have given some thought to what you will be doing when you are sixty-four. I haven't, and I certainly don't expect to be climbing mountains, but life expectancy keeps growing (70), especially for women, so who knows?

I don't suppose that when Kuwabara-san was my age she had any thought of being an alpinist when she was sixty-four, either. She and her husband had a family business of some sort in Tokyo. When the husband died early in 1971, her older son was still unmarried and she went into partnership with him to continue the business. She had two other sons and two daughters, one of them married, which is a very large family by today's standards. (I don't know anybody anymore with a family as big as ours was in Yonago.)

Kuwabara-san had never been athletic as a girl the way Yoko-san and I were. (Did I tell you that Tamiko-san's P.T.A. volley ball team won the Omiya citywide championship? They were quickly eliminated playing against another team for the prefecture championship, however.) In Kuwabara-san's day, girls did not participate in athletics, and her parents had even scolded her when she tried to learn to ride a bicycle. What she did like was to paint *haiga* [black and white *brushwork related to haiku*, the short Japanese poetic form]. When she saw a newspaper story about a mountain-climbing club for people over forty, it occurred to her that it might be interesting to go off into the mountains, since so many *haiku* are concerned with nature, so she joined. She read the literature they sent her, but she had never gone anywhere on her own while she was married. So she was hesitant about going to an unfamiliar subway station and meeting a group of strangers, and she put off any actual participation in the organization.

Finally, in the spring of 1974, she received a telephone call from a woman in her district who had seen her name in the membership list of the mountaineering organization and wondered why she did not join the group on one of its hikes. So in early April 1974, at age fifty-eight, she took a knapsack and windbreaker that had belonged to her older daughter, got up very early in the morning, met the group at Takao station, about an hour outside Tokyo, and climbed Takao-san [Mount Takao].

That first climb was a revelation to her. She enjoyed the beauty of nature, she liked the companionship, and she went on to make four more climbs that year, each one more difficult than the last. The following year, her oldest son was married and took over the family business, but his bride was not able to assume the business responsibilities that Kuwabara-san had been handling, and the son went home at night leaving a lot of work for Kuwabara-san to do in addition to her housekeeping duties. This led to a good deal of bickering between mother and son, which so depressed Kuwabara-san that she became ill. She had a country house and thought it might be best if she went to live there, but a friend said she would be unhappy out of town and far away from her friends so she persuaded her son to live in the country house and commute to work while she kept the Tokyo house. One of her daughters suggested that she resume her mountain-climbing, which she did.

In the peace and stillness of the mountains, she found that people could open their hearts and have an honest exchange of feelings without fear of scandal. Many other older people had problems with their sons and daughters-in-law very much like her own, she discovered. So she continued her mountain-climbing and went on to scale about two hundred peaks, including Okuhodaka, Yarigadake, Tsurugadake, and others in the Kita Alps [Japanese Alps] that are difficult even for much younger people.

A Waseda University mountain-climbing group announced that it was going to the Himalayas this year and invited Kuwabara-san to join. Her children tried to discourage her, and she had doubts herself, so it was not until almost the last moment that she decided to go. There were twenty-two people in the group, including students, graduates, and professors. Kuwabara-san and the sixty-five year old woman physician I mentioned were the oldest. They all flew from Narita Airport to New Delhi, took another airline to Srinagar in Kashmir, and proceeded to the base of the mountain, where they were met by Sherpa guides. Each of the younger climbers had a research project of some sort. The two older women thought they would have a hard time just to keep up, much less pursue any research, but it turned out that they were the last to feel the ill effects of the thin air at the higher altitudes. The young women students were affected first. The older women thought that their resistance might be based on the fact that they had endured hardships during the war and had learned to survive with little food.

The group slept in tents for two weeks, camping beside streams. Most of the climbers drank water without first boiling it, so almost all of them developed stomach problems. Everyone made it to the top except one person who had developed a fever as part of the altitude sickness. Kuwabara-san lost five kilograms on the expedition, but she came through like a veteran climber. When we celebrate *Keiro no hi* [Respect for Old People Day] September 15 and entertain people of seventy and over (In some places it's still sixty-five and over) at the community center for lunch, many of us will think of Kuwabara-san.

I'm sure Hiroshi Okura, the head of Noevir, is excited about Kuwabara-san's accomplishment since he used to be such an ardent mountain climber himself. In fact, he tells Noevir representatives like me that being successful in business is like climbing a mountain. It may look impossible, but research and a good effort and some determination combine to make it possible. He tells us to forget the word "impossible." He says that if you think about the cold and lack of oxygen and all the other obstacles, you will never try to reach the moon, yet man *has* reached the moon. I know, people are always saying that if we could reach the moon we certainly ought to be able to solve a lot of problems here on earth that continue to go unsolved, but Okura-san insists that if we just use our God-given abilities and are hungry enough, we will find solutions. We just have to work at it.

Most of the top men in Japanese government and in the big companies here are in their sixties and seventies. Okura-san thinks that will change, because even though a lot of the *genro* [elder men] are still hale and hearty, there is a lot of what we call old-age pollution and it is still news when a man in his fifties becomes the president of a big company.

On one hand, people argue that Japanese business will lose its dynamic quality if it is dominated by old men who have the illusion that nothing will happen without them around. On the other hand, I understand that the Sony Walkman is very popular in America, and that idea evidently came from the honorary chairman of Sony, Masaru Ibuka, who is hardly a young man. With the drop in the birthrate, Japan has become an aging society, they say. And despite the fact that the retirement age for men who don't become directors is generally fifty-five, or at most sixty, the working population now has an abnormally high percentage of people over sixty-five.

I don't know how it is now, but after the first oil shock in the early 1970s many older men were laid off, and although the *taishokukin* [lump sum retirement pay] that they received seemed like a lot of money, we had high inflation at the time and the money did not go as far as it once would have. Also, many men were not careful about how they invested their *taishokukin*, and they had to go back to work. The trouble was that there were eight or ten applicants for every job available at the employment offices for older men, and most of the jobs were too difficult or too poorly paid to interest younger men. Older men still take jobs as guards, janitors, highway toll collectors, and so forth, but about half of them quit within a year because the work is too hard.

So many men spend their lives working for the company, and when they are retired they don't know what to do with themselves. A woman can take care of herself no matter how old she is, provided that she can move about, but men have been treated as masters and haven't any idea how to cook or look after their own needs. We are very lucky that *Oto-o-san* has our stepmother to take care of him. They say that the *kakukazoku* [nuclear family] is replacing the traditional extended family, but the government issued a report recently showing that most older men in this country live with their children or grandchildren. That is not true of old women, but it is true of old men (71). Of course, if an older person lives alone here, people think he or she must be disagreeable or that the younger generation must be stingy or selfish. On the other hand, the suicide rate is higher among older people living with their children or grandchildren than among older people living alone. There have been cases of double suicide because the wife became ill and the husband could not face life without her. You wrote about the welfare workers that New York City sends to help older people who are sick or disabled. Our welfare system is not very good, and that is unheard of. Old people are dependent upon their children, and when the children shut them out, which happens quite a lot, there are problems. There are always stories in the paper about old people being found dead in their houses or apartments because nobody in the family was looking after them or was even in touch with them.

Years ago, not so many people lived for so long and we are still not prepared to deal with the situation. We respect our old people, but we don't really know what to do with them, and many are very lonely. Some of them buy life-size dolls. Although the dolls were originally designed for children, they have become popular among old people who have been left without children or grandchildren. We don't have many elderly people in this community but there is at least one that I have seen occasionally who takes her doll, all dressed in fine woolens, to the playground and shares a gently moving swing with her make-believe grandchild.

Old people are not the only lonely ones. I think that our social traditions tend to isolate people, especially now that families are smaller, and sometimes I suspect that part of the success of door-to-door and home party salespeople, such as Noevir Ladies, is that there are so many lonely women who just want somebody to talk to.

My Noevir wholesaler tells me that her ambition is to open a retirement home for Noevir Ladies when she gets old so that they will never have to be lonely or dependent upon their families. Meanwhile, she wants to make enough money to have her own building. She says it would include various beauty shops (For the hair, the skin, and so forth) plus a boutique — everything to enhance the female animal, she says, which is not very delicately put, perhaps, but is straightforward. She has six top distributors like me plus nearly seventy second level distributors, and she takes us out to dinner at a restaurant occasionally. Hajime has dinner at Yoko-san's house on those evenings.

The emphasis in Japan is still on youth, and we still spoil our children, especially our sons, although I try not to pamper Hajime the way some boys are pampered. Hajime and the others have been working to clean up the streets and the little park, such as it is. School reopens tomorrow, and the children have ended their vacation with the traditional clean-up week.

Sachiko

20 September

Dear Chie,

Well, I have taken the leap and have become a wholesaler. I told you that I had been thinking about it, and my wholesaler, Hanako Taketomo, finally persuaded me that I should. Most of the wholesalers are men, but Taketomo-san does better than some men and she says I could, too. We shall see.

The whole idea of having wholesalers compete with each other comes from Okura-san. His philosophy is that the traditional Japanese business system of promoting people on the basis of seniority cannot last, and I think he is right. After all, our companies have to compete with other companies, and not only with other Japanese companies. Those that succeed are generally the ones that deliver the best products and services, and that's the way it should be with people in a company. Somebody who contributes a lot should be rewarded, and while there is some of that in Japanese companies, promotions are still based primarily on seniority, not merit. We operate according to the old principle *deru kugi wa tatakareru* [the nail that sticks out gets hammered down], which discourages people from asserting themselves and competing. I think people like to compete. We grow up competing in sports, and it's fun. A lot of people don't realize how much fun some business people have competing. Not that it's all a game, but it does have some aspects that are like scoring points in a game.

I realize, of course, that Okura-san's purpose in encouraging competition is to boost overall sales, and I realize that Taketomo-san's purpose in wanting me to be a distributor is to boost her own income, since she gets a percentage of all my sales. In one sense I will competing with her, and in another sense I will still be working for her, but the way Okura-san has it set up, what she makes out of my office's revenues will come from the company, not directly out of my office.

Please forgive me for talking so much about my business, but we had our big annual meeting at the Tokyo Prince Hotel (there are other such meetings in other parts of the country this month). and it was not like anything I had ever attended before. Some distributors were awarded prizes for their success. I was not one of them, but I enjoyed the reception afterward. There were about eleven hundred people, mostly women, with live music and an elegant buffet. I didn't know what to wear and ended up wearing my best kimono. I bought a new *obi* [silken waist band worn with kimono], which cost more than forty thousand yen [two hundred dollars] but was cheaper than some at the store. I noticed quite a few others in kimono, but many of the women wore Western evening gowns, some of them designer gowns. Functions like these are usually just for men, and if there are any women present they do not talk much among themselves. This was very different. I got to meet women from as far away as Sapporo and some of them had really helpful ideas about recruiting Noevir Ladies. Everyone I met had originally been a housewife just like me, and each one had developed business methods all her own. It was very interesting, and I realized that women are adaptable by nature. When a woman has her first child, she may get advice and read books about infant care, but since every child is different every mother has to develop means of dealing with her own individual child, and just about every woman does. That's the way it is in business. A woman may not think she can do it, but she finds a way.

Also, I finally got a chance to meet Okura-san in person, which was a thrill. He has the warmest smile and a very friendly manner — rather boyish, really, and quite charming. He doesn't smoke, and he told me that he doesn't let anyone in his office smoke, which surprised me. He said it was silly for a woman to use perfume or cologne and then to spoil her scent with the smell of cigarette smoke. Some of his ideas are so bold and unconventional that you would expect him to be youthful rather than the typical *genro* that is usually at the head of a big company, and he certainly is youthful. He has a pleasant informality, yet his enthusiasm for what we are doing is so great that you can see why he has been so successful. Whether or not my own career as a wholesaler will be very successful remains to be seen, but I have made two of my number two distributors number one distributors and have made my three best Noevir Ladies number two distributors.

One of them has already signed up six new Noevir Ladies. The way she did it was rather ingenious, I think. She figured that young mothers with children in kindergarten might have a special interest in becoming Noevir Ladies, so she went to the local kindergarten, got the names of the mothers, and approached each one.

Being a wholesaler should produce more money for me, but it will also require that I keep more money in the bank for credit reasons, and I'll have to rent a bigger office than the one I've had as a distributor, which means that we will have to postpone buying a house a little longer. I hope it also means that when we do buy a house it can be a better one than it would have been otherwise. Toshiro-san agrees that we should wait. He sends you his regards.

Sachiko

27 December

Dear Chie,

It has been ages since I wrote and you must think I'm terrible. The truth is that being a wholesaler takes more time than I had expected and sometimes more than I would like. It has meant a lot of changes for all of us, the biggest change being that we now live in a house of our own. I think I may have written that we were going to postpone buying a house because I had to keep a lot of money in the bank and I needed a bigger office. Well, one of Toshiro-san's associates, or actually the number two man in a company that is a major supplier to Toshiro-san's company, had to leave Tokyo. His father died and he was needed to take over the family business in Osaka. Toshiro-san heard the story and told me about the man's house, so before the man could put his house on the market Toshiro-san and I looked at it and made an offer, which was accepted.

The house is not too far from where we live now but in a slightly older section, and it is just large enough to have room for my office without having it intrude on the privacy of the house itself. Creating the office required some construction work, which is now completed, and it all feels very luxurious after living in the apartment for so long. There is even a garage and a little garden.

We were extremely lucky to find such a house, and although the price was far more than I had ever expected to pay, people tell us we got a bargain. There have been frightening reports on television and in the newspapers about families having to give up houses because they could not afford to keep up the payments, and then having to continue making payments for several years because no new buyer could be found right away. It all made Toshiro-san very nervous, but I assured him that the loan from his company plus the money I am making as a wholesaler would be more than enough to keep us safe from anything like that.

What it will take to improve the housing situation here is hard to say. Toshiro-san tells me that part of the trouble comes from the fact that so much money is wasted on public works. The projects all cost more than they should because the construction companies find ways to get around competitive bidding. They make big campaign contributions to politicians, so nobody stops the corruption. The Seikan (Aomori-Hakodate) undersea tunnel to Hokkaido is nearly completed now, yet there is still no definite plan for its use. There are big plans to build bridges across the Seto Inland Sea to connect Honshu with Shikoku, to extend the *Shinkansen* [bullet train] lines to the northern part of the country, and to build a new Kansai airport. I think the more pressing need is to build housing, so while I am happy that our own housing situation has been so happily resolved, I still feel bad about the situation in general.

When Toshiro-san told me about the house, he asked me to go along when he met with the owner to discuss the matter. I picked him up at his office, which I had not done for ten years, and we had lunch together, just the two of us, which is something else we had not done for a long, long while. (My assistant ran my office that day.) Earlier, I had bought Toshiro-san a beautiful new wristwatch (You may remember that his old one was not keeping good time), and when he came back from the washroom the jewelry store box was beside his glass of beer.

When he arrives home in the evening now I can sense a difference in his manner. For my own part, I feel a freshness that I have not experienced in years, a feeling of excitement that reminds me of how it was when we were just dating, and I know Toshiro-san feels the same way. He didn't say anything that first evening except that his colleagues had teased him about how they could understand why he was always hurrying home to see his wife. I have to dress better for my business, and I did look rather smart when I picked him up at his office. What really has changed in our relationship, though, is that we now talk more openly about so many things than we did when I was just a housewife. Not that I think there is anything wrong with being just a housewife, but it was never enough for me, and Toshiro-san realizes that.

I think that the owner of the house was surprised that Toshiro-san had brought his wife along to participate in the discussion. It is not usual, and it is a sign that things are changing at least in the way some men regard women.

Looking ahead to the new year, I can see that my life will be quite different. You have been such a help to me, Chie-san. I can remember how you took care of me when our mother was not well, and I have always looked up to you as someone that was more than just an older sister. Perhaps if you had lived next door I might not have felt free to say some of the things that I have written to you. The fact that you are so far away has given you a special dimension and has made it easier in some ways for me to be open with you. As I say, your replies have been very warm and supportive, and I don't know who else could have been so helpful and reassuring. You have not only told me a lot about America but have helped me to understand a lot about myself as a woman in Japan.

I have been amused by things that you have told me about feminist attitudes in America. Here, of course, we are just as happy not to mix in our husbands' business affairs and not to have our husbands encroach on our own territory. It might be nice to have men wait to let us enter elevators first, or to have waiters serve us before the men, or to feel as free as you are to express opinions instead of agreeing — or at least seeming to agree — with the men, but we like our formalities, including the fact that there are feminine ways to say certain things and masculine ways (72), even though that may be based on the old Confucian male supremacy idea. Perhaps some women do not like it; I don't mind, any more than I mind that women cover their mouths when they laugh while men never do. Anyway, those things are not about to change, and rather than waste a lot of energy trying to change them I think we will do better to work for more meaningful gains. Women are making progress here, even though the mass media continues to extoll women who sacrifice themselves for their families. The newspaper and TV news editors act as if they were the defenders of the old Confucian view of women as housekeepers, child-raisers, and men-pleasers. They don't seem to realize how much some women want to break that mold. I met a young woman reporter from the *Mainichi Shimbun* who told me that she had been chosen from among three hundred women applicants, so you can see that journalism is still a male preserve.

Okura-san, the head of Noevir, says that women have more patience, better judgment, and more courage than men, especially men in smaller towns and cities. He says that is partly because it takes those qualities to bear and raise children, and partly because men with ambition and ability leave for better opportunities in the big cities, so among the people who remain the women tend to be smarter and more aggressive than the men. My own self-confidence has grown enormously in the past two years, and while I can hardly expect everything to go smoothly at all times, I feel that I will be able to manage as well as anyone. Our correspondence may suffer somewhat on account of the business, which will take up more and more of my time for a few years, but I did want you to know how much your letters have meant to me.

Any visit to America will have to be put off still further, I'm afraid, and I'm sure that you will come here to see us again before we can ever get over there to see you, although I still yearn to see your Central Park. Toshiro-san and Hajime join me in wishing you and James-san a happy new year full of health and good fortune.

Sachiko

NOTES

1. Fusae Ichikawa was born in 1893 and was eighty-seven when she died in February 1981, two days before she was to receive an award from the government for her twenty-five years of service to the country as a senator in the National Diet. Ichikawa was the daughter of a poor farmer, and at a time when only forty percent of Japanese girls even went to elementary school, she somehow managed to go through high school and attend a teacher's college. She taught elementary school, became a newspaper reporter in Aichi Prefecture, and eventually went to Tokyo. As a child, Ichikawa had seen her father abuse his wife for no apparent reason and was painfully aware that women in her country were second-class citizens, unable to vote, prevented by law from forming organizations, unable to inherit property, without rights even to their own children in the event of divorce or the death of their husbands.

In 1919, Ichikawa defied the law and started the organization New Women (*Atarashi Onna*) with Raicho Hiratsuka, the main figure in Japan's pioneer women's rights movement, the Bluestockings. Hiratsuka, whose first name was really Haru, was the daughter of a man who had helped draft the Japanese Constitution promulgated in 1889 and the civil code whose provisions were so heavily weighted against women. When she was twenty-five, Hiratsuka started a literary magazine, *Seito*, or *Bluestocking*, which began publication at Tokyo in September 1911. The Shinto sun god *Amaterasuomikami* is a woman, and Hiratsuka wrote in that first issue, "In the beginning, women were the sun. The sun was shining, and we were truly human beings. Now we are the moon, pale-faced like sick people, shining only as the reflection of others. We must take back our hidden sun. We must find our hidden talents...." *Seito* was suppressed after its February 1916 issue.

Raicho Hiratsuka's mother, Tsuya, was a physician's daughter who had married at age seventeen. As the wife of a man in Japan's elite upper class she had to know how to dance, sing, play the piano or violin, make Western clothes, do embroidery, knit, know about current literature, and carry on a conversation using fashionable vocabulary. After their first child was born, her husband sent her to school, letting his mother take care of the child. There were no Japanese colleges for women at that time so he sent her to Sakurai

Jojuku, a small school for girls that later became a college. She studied English at that school and then went to Hitotsubashi, a vocational school for girls. Tsuya's husband believed in education for women so long as it did not go too far, and he was somewhat shaken when his wife went behind his back to help finance their daughter's defiance of the civil code. The daughter married a man five years her junior but refused to register the marriage, since it would have meant forfeiting all rights to her husband. When she had first one child and then another, she had them registered under her own name. Her husband testified that the children were his and were not illegitimate, he supported his wife in insisting that the children be registered under her name, the government maintained that the couple was not legally married, and there was a big fight before the issue was resolved in her Hiratsuka's favor. In fact, the marriage lasted fifty years.

As for the organization New Women, *Atarashii Onna* became an obscene term among Japanese men and stones were thrown at Raicho Hiratsuka's house. Like suffragist movements in Britain and America, the movement produced martyrs; still it continued, and one of its leaders was Fusae Ichikawa. In 1929, Ichikawa came to the United States, where she remained for three years. When she returned to Japan, she organized a confederation to agitate for female suffrage, but right-wing forces were taking over the country, proclaiming the Great East Asia Co-Prosperity Sphere, and seeking military solutions to the economic depression that afflicted Japan as it did the rest of the world. Japanese women who supported the right-wing government formed a patriotic organization — *Aikoku Fujinkai*. In 1937, Japan invaded China; four years later, Japanese forces attacked the U.S. naval base at Pearl Harbor in Hawaii and began pouring troops into Southeast Asia, the Philippines, and the Dutch East Indies.

When the war finally ended in 1945, Fusae Ichikawa organized the Confederation of New Japanese Women. Its objectives included clean elections and political education for women. The Japanese government had been planning to give women the right to vote even before General Douglas MacArthur's administration imposed a new constitution which contained that right. The Japanese election law allowed companies to make political contributions. Ichikawa fought without success to have the law changed so that only individual contributions would be permitted, thus cutting the links between business and government. When she campaigned for office, she made incorruptibility such an issue that aides had to bring their own lunches. Although the law allowed candidates to spend a certain amount for campaign expenses, Ichikawa usually spent only twenty to thirty percent of what was permitted. She refused a medal that Emperor Hirohito wanted to confer upon her and the only award she ever accepted was one from the newspaper *Asahi Shimbun*, which in January 1973 honored Ichikawa for her contributions to the progress of women in Japan and to the political education of all qualified voters. In accepting the award, she said that women should be more independent and should make their own choices, that they should be brave and fight for their rights even when they were afraid of losing their jobs.

Japan elects senators on the basis both of nationwide and pre-fecturewide voting (a prefecture is comparable to an American state). In 1980, at age eighty-six, Ichikawa received more votes nationwide than any other candidate for the *Sangiin*, the upper house of the National Diet. She organized a conference in 1980 of forty-eight women's organizations ranging from radical to con-servative, and it was generally acknowledged that nobody else could have done it except Ichikawa, who was almost universally known and widely respected.

2. *Onnadaigaku*, a booklet by students of the Confucianist philos-opher-teacher Ekiken Kaibara (1630-1714), contains ethical princi-ples with regard to women (*onna* is Japanese for female; *daigaku* is Japanese for teaching). Until the end of the Kamakura period (1185-1333), a Japanese woman inherited her husband's property at his death and took full responsibility for his obligations. By the time of the Tokugawa period (1600-1868), the rights of women were almost non-existent. An official proclamation by the Tokugawa govern-ment in 1649 decreed that a farmer must divorce his wife, no matter how attractive she was, if she did not get up very early in the morning, did not go out and collect hay to feed the livestock, did not work in the rice fields during the day, did not make rope or rice containers from rice straw in the evening, did not take good care of her husband, did her work carelessly, drank too much tea, or took too much time for leisure.

Under the principles outlined in *Onnadaigaku*, men and women were kept apart beginning at age seven, and marriages were arranged. A marriage not condoned by the parents was considered an adulterous relationship and to be considered virtuous, a woman had to be obedient and submissive. Women with ability, brains, or talent were regarded as troublesome. Until she was married, a woman had to obey her father; then she had to obey her husband; and after her husband's death she had to obey her oldest son. She was expected to be good at weaving, sewing, cooking, and washing. Above all, she was a child-producing machine. Professor Edwin O. Reischauer of Harvard was U.S. Ambassador to Japan from 1961 to 1966 and has a Japanese wife. In his 1977 book *The Japanese*, Professor Reischauer wrote, "The primitive Japanese revered fertility not just in agriculture but among humans as well, and phallic symbols were common objects of worship in rural Japan until recent times. In the classical period, love became the main literary theme in a court life of astonishingly free sexual ways. Some of this sexual freedom survived into modern times in parts of rural Japan, where premarital sexual relations were condoned and marriages were frequently not registered, and therefore not made permanent, until the bride had proven her ability to bear children." Even in more conventional marriages, the wife's duty was to bear children that would carry on the family bloodline. If a wife could not bear children she was expected to leave, although she might be permitted to remain if she was good-natured and if her husband was able to sire a child by a mistress. If she did not leave, she was expected to adopt the child of one of her husband's relatives. A husband could divorce his wife if she was unable to bear children. He could also divorce her if she was immoral, if she continually argued with her in-laws, if she talked too much, if she was dishonest, or jealous, or diseased. According to the principles of *Onnadaigaku*, a woman had no lord other than her husband; it was her duty to serve him and never to criticize or disparage, only to obey. Having many children by a wife or by mistresses was a mark of masculinity in Japan (as in many Latin countries). Even in modern times a Japanese woman had virtually no rights, including the right to complain if her husband patronized brothels. She was even expected to pay his brothel bills.

A Japanese law enacted in 1870 established two kinds of kinship: kinship between parent and child was kinship of the first degree; kinship between husband and wife or *between husband and mistress* was kinship in the second degree, and a man was permitted to have as many mistresses as he could afford. Two years later, in 1872, a book by the founder of Keio University criticized the law permitting mistresses to belong to a man's household and to have rights comparable to those of his wife. Yukichi Fukuda urged strict monogomy. His supporters were called *Meirokusha*, and in 1880 they succeeded in having the law changed so that relationships with mistresses were no longer officially recognized, but many men, including the emperor, continued to take mistresses. Famous *geishas* sometimes became mistresses to rich noblemen. When the Meiji emperor Mutsuhito died in 1912 at age sixty after a forty-five-year reign, it was rumored that his son Yoshihito, who succeeded as the emperor Taisho, was the son not of the emperor's wife but of a mistress. (Taisho was not altogether stable, and his son Hirohito, who succeeded him in 1926, had been acting as regent for five years at the time of his father's death.) Adultery under the old code was punishable in the case of wives but a husband could be punished only if his sexual partner were somebody else's wife and the woman's husband took the matter to court.

Until 1871, intermarriage among certain Japanese social classes was not permitted. The *shi* (*samurai*), the *no* (farmers), the *ko* (craftsmen), and the *sho* (merchants) were kept separate, and the groups were distinguished by different clothing, different food, different houses, and different ways of speaking. Anyone who violated the separation of classes was thought to endanger the entire social system. Intermarriage with the outcaste *Eta*, who lived in special villages and worked at unclean jobs that involved animals, such as tanning leather, was expressly forbidden. By 1871, many *samurai* (*see* note 37) were very poor and in a number of cases had sold their titles to merchants or rich farmers, who thus became *samurai* themselves. After 1871, any girl could be married to a *samurai*. As with all Japanese wives, any money or property the *samurai*'s wife inherited went automatically to him. As with all Japanese wives, her children belonged to her husband's family; if he died, or if they were divorced, the children went to the family and the wife had no rights to them. So long as her husband's mother was alive, the mother could order her son to divorce his wife. The son often turned his pay over to his mother, not to his wife, and it was the mother who decided how the money was to be spent. This relationship between mother, son, and daughter-in-law continued under the civil code that was operative until after World War II. A couple that wanted to get married had to obtain permission from all four parents and from the head of each household, the *koshu*, who might be a grandfather but was in any case a man. Nobody could be married into the family, or adopted by anyone in the household, or divorced without the *koshu*'s permission. If anyone disobeyed the *koshu*, he could disown them or withhold support. For his part, the *koshu* was obligated to support his grandparents, his parents, his wife, his children, and his siblings, and to provide the children with an education.

Under the terms of a law passed in 1873, a woman without a son could be the *koshu* on a temporary basis until she married a man who would adopt her family name (such husbands even now are called *muko-iri*, meaning that they "enter the family") or until her daughter found a *muko*. In 1878, a widow named Kita Kasuse in Kochi Prefecture, Shikoku, went to vote in a local election, insisting that she was the *koshu* of her household and a taxpayer. She was told that only men could vote, and this was justified on the ground that men served in the military. Kasuse pointed out that *koshu* did not have to serve, nor did oldest sons, but she was still not permitted to vote. When her tax notice arrived, she refused to pay and wrote to the Ministry of the Interior. A story about Kasuse appeared in the newspaper *Tokyo Nichinichi Shimbun* January 31, 1879, and although the paper called her an eccentric woman, she gained fame as the *minken oba-a-san*, or civil rights grandmother. As recently as 1946, a Japanese wife could represent her husband but could not own property; the husband controlled his wife's property, even if she had inherited it from her family.

In some other respects, Japanese society was always a matriarchy. The main section of a classic Japanese house was the *omoya* (*omo* — mother, *ya* — house). Mother held the pursestrings. Having once been a daughter-in-law herself, she determined whether her daughter-in-law was worthy of her son. At the beginning of the Showa period that started with the emperor Hirohito (1926-), a writer observed that the mother of the mayor of To-ono, a village in Iwate

Prefecture, ordered her son to go out before breakfast to feed the livestock and ordered her daughter-in-law to feed the horses. While the son was the *koshu*, the mother was still the head of the household, the *shakushiken* or *hera-mochi* (both words mean the one with the right to hold the spoon used to serve rice).

Even today, the relationship between a wife and her mother-in-law tends to be a difficult one in Japan, far more than in Western countries. Fewer young people live with the husband's parents after marriage, given the present housing shortage, so the tradition is weakening, but it is still strong. When a daughter-in-law herself becomes a mother-in-law, she exercises the privileges of the *hera-mochi* and makes her son's wife endure something of what she once had to endure. In other respects, even under the constitution that permits women to inherit money and own property, Japanese society remains a patriarchy. If a man has daughters but no sons, one of the daughters, especially an only daughter, may be married to a *muko* who will agree to accept his wife's name and thus carry on the father's family name.

3. *Pachinko* is Japanese-style pinball, played with steel balls (one hundred yen dropped into a slot will yield about a hundred balls) of the sort used in ball-bearings on machines with vertical boards that take up less space than American pinball machines. In countless *pachinko* parlors, addicted (there is no other word) Japanese of both sexes and all ages spend countless hours sitting or standing in solitary, mesmerized absorption as they watch the balls go up and around the board, disappearing into little holes or multiplying in clattering jubilation as the player scores.

4. The medal was evidently awarded to men of the emperor's own age. Chie's father worked for JNR (Japanese National Railways) from 1918 until his retirement in 1956 and kept the superannuated trains running at times when it was virtually impossible to obtain spare parts, improvising repairs, and training competent mechanics. I have teased Chie with the suggestion that her father received the medal for helping win the war.

Before the war, the emperor gave medals to people for good citizenship. The practice began in 1882 and there were four kinds of ribbons: the red *koju* medal was for saving someone's life at the risk of one's own; the green *ryokuju* medal was for virtuous women who had served their husbands or their parents above and beyond the call of duty. This medal was also given to servants who had been especially faithful to their masters and to people whose behavior had been exemplary; the blue *ranju* medal was for people whose work had benefited the public and whose record of public service had been outstanding; it was awarded mostly to people in government service. From 1882 to 1897, only one of the six hundred and eighteen people who received *koju* medals was a woman, and only two women received *ranju* medals; twenty-seven of the two hundred and three *ryokuju* medal recipients were women. One of these was Toku Komagata of Niigata Prefecture who had attracted public attention during the so-called *Nisshinsenso*, the Sino-Japanese War of 1894-1895, by telling the government that she wanted to donate one yen for the war effort and then working night and day to earn the one yen. Betrothed in 1860 at age twenty, she discovered that her fiance's family had lost most of its property and had barely enough to eat. She was advised not to go through with the marriage but replied that she had given her word. It then developed that her husband's older brother was retarded and dependent upon her blacksmith husband, that the men's mother was arthritic and unable to take care of herself much less work, and that the father had a hot temper. In order to take care of her in-laws, she had to sleep beside them at night, not even removing her *obi* [the sash a woman wears about her kimono]. Working harder than any man while she raised six children, Komagata was up before dawn and had to work by candle-light at night, spinning, weaving, cooking, cleaning, working in the fields in summer, raising silkworms, collecting firewood in winter. After her parents-in-law died, she had to take care of her brother-in-law. When her husband became ill, she had to nurse him, and when he died she did not remarry. Her second and third sons joined the army, and the Meiji government, which gave her a medal in March 1897, considered her an example for all Japanese women.

5. *Juku* is special academic coaching to help students get good grades and prepare them for junior high school, high school, or college. As many as fifty children may be in one elementary school

classroom, and since children are never allowed to skip or repeat grades, the speed of instruction is paced to slightly below-average children. *Juku* classes are held twice a week, on average, and a *juku* often rents some university classrooms on Sundays and national holidays. Only about five percent of first graders attend *juku*; by sixth grade, as much as twenty-seven percent of the class may be attending, largely to fulfill their mothers' (and sometimes fathers') ambitions.

The pressure to do well in school stems from the Japanese business system in which very large companies dominate the economic scene. These large companies — and government agencies as well — recruit men (plus a few women these days) almost exclusively from the state-supported Imperial Universities, especially Tokyo University — which accept only ninety-six thousand students each year out of some seven hundred thousand high school graduates — and the elite private universities. Some men today get good jobs with big companies without having graduated from the right college, but that is still rare. A major company tends to hire from a specific university, and that university may accept most of its freshmen from a specific high school. Some prestigious private universities, such as Keio University, may have their own high schools, junior highs, elementary schools, and even kindergartens, so if parents wish a son to work for a given company they may have to start planning from before kindergarten to get the boy into the high school that will get him into the right college for the company of their choice.

More than sixty-five percent of Japanese high school students pursue college entrance curricula even though only thirty-two percent of high school graduates go on to college. Having to go to into a technical curriculum is evidence of failure to succeed in an academic curriculum and brings loss of face. Beginning with kindergarten, Japanese educational institutions have fiercely rigorous entrance examinations. High school students aiming for college virtually all take the same courses, using similar textbooks turned out by the three textbook publishing houses, so a student is judged entirely on his or her performance on the entrance examination. Rich and poor compete on an equal basis, but parents who can afford it try to give their children a competitive edge, typically paying the equivalent of fifty to seventy-five dollars per month for *juku* classes (three two-hour classes per week will generally cost the equivalent of about seventy dollars per month).

Going to a top high school will make a student better prepared for university entrance examinations. Going to a top private junior high school will help a student obtain admission to a top private high school. Attending a top private elementary school will make it easier to enter a top junior high school. To get into a top private elementary school, a child must have gone to a good kindergarten, and some Japanese kindergartens accept only one out of eighteen or twenty applicants. Which is why parents spend as much as a thousand dollars per week to have their children drilled for eight hours a day, six days per week, in special pre-kindergarten summer schools. Through elementary school and high school, a boy's *juku* fees may cost the family several hundred dollars per month.

Officially, Japan has a six-three-three school system, with six years in elementary school, three in junior high, and three in senior high. In practice, it is a six-two-one-two-one system, with the last year in junior high and the last in senior high devoted exclusively to preparation for the entrance examinations to get into higher schools. In the weeks after the New Year holidays, normal instruction goes on for students planning to take jobs after graduation and for those assured of university enrollment on the basis of recommendations. Ordinary classes are dissolved for students preparing themselves for entrance examinations. These students receive intensive lessons in mathematics, English, or other subjects, depending on the kind of tests to be given by the universities they hope to enter. Some young people crack under the pressure. For those who can stand up to the rigors of *shiken jigoku* (examination hell), and who can persevere to the point of getting into a desirable university, a good future is virtually assured. The American with a bachelor's degree from Harvard, Wellesley, Yale, Vassar, Princeton, Smith, Columbia, Stamford, Pennsylvania, or Chicago may find opportunities not available to others, and the vistas are even brighter for Tokyo University graduates.

With the percentage of young Japanese going to college now comparable to the percentage in the United States, a bachelor's degree is not worth what it once was, and, just as in the United

States, there has been a growing tendency for majors in the humanities to re-enroll as science or engineering majors (Japan graduates more engineers each year than does the United States, yet there are never enough) and for bachelors of law and economics to acquire skills as electricians, automobile mechanics, gardeners, or craftsmen, but there is always a demand for graduates of Tokyo University. While money cannot buy entrance to an elite university, if a student has some ability it can be developed with the proper financial support, and it is easy to see why Japanese families of means consider education a worthwhile investment of time and effort.

When compulsory education began in August 1872, education was not free (high school is still not free). Monthly tuition was fifteen to twenty-five sen at a time when a hundred sen (one yen) could buy two *to*, nine *sho* (about fifty-seven quarts) of rice. Poor people were hard pressed to pay, and girls were considered better off without education, which was actually thought harmful to women. A poor family and sometimes even a middle class family sent its daughters off to work as maids in respectable households where they could learn how to behave in polite society and prepare themselves for marriage and motherhood. A girl had to know how to spin, weave, sew, cook, wash, and take care of children. It was thought that any further education would simply make a girl unhappy, so relatively few girls showed up at the girls schools that opened in 1872. In 1873, forty-six percent of the eligible boys came to elementary school but only sixteen percent of the eligible girls. Four years later, fifty-four percent of the eligible boys were attending elementary school but only thirty-three percent of the eligible girls. Japanese girls began attending school in the United States in 1871. Of the five girls in the first group, the youngest was eight-year-old Umeko Tsuda. When she returned to Japan ten years later, she had forgotten her Japanese. She subsequently founded Tsuda Eigaku-juku to teach English to Japanese girls, and Tokyo's Tsuda Girls' College is an outgrowth of that English school.

Japan's first private university was Keio University, which began with a Tokyo school founded by Yukichi Fukuzawa. Fukuzawa's revolutionary book *An Encouragement of Learning* (*Gakumon no susume*) was a best seller in 1872, with sales of nearly three and a half million copies. It began with the words, "Heaven created no man above another, and no man below another," which contradicted Confucian philosophy, and it included a chapter on women. Fukuzawa, in fact, criticized the *Onnadaigaku's* view (*see* note 2) of women's education, saying that the world could not exist without both men and women, that women were just as human as men.

On the advice of one David Murray, an American or Englishman who worked for the Ministry of Education, the Ministry founded a teachers school for women in the Ochanomizu (the word means water for tea) district of Tokyo. The school opened in late November 1875 but had trouble finding girls who were qualified to be, and desirous of being, schoolteachers. When Japan's first girls' high school opened in 1882, it taught mostly sewing, housekeeping, and poise. It became a public school operated by the government in 1886, but the emphasis was still on how to be a good wife. In a girl's final year, she was given instruction on how to relate to a husband and a mother-in-law, how to raise children, how to keep house, how to treat servants, and how to behave in society. How little that has changed. As Edwin O. Reischauer wrote in *The Japanese*, "Though the majority of junior college students are women, these colleges are looked upon, in a sense, as finishing schools, preparing women with polite accomplishments for marriage. At the four-year university level, women decline sharply in numbers. As recently as 1950 they accounted for only 2 percent of univesity students. There are a few women's universities, largely of Christian background, but in the other universities, all of which are now coeducational, women constitute only about a fifth of the student population and a mere 10 percent in the best institutions. An expensive four year university education seems less worthwhile for girls, who are expected to end up as no more than housewives."

With most women having no more than one or two children today, each child is the focus of more effort on the part of parents and one often hears the term *Kyoiku mama*, or education mother, for a woman who pushes her child to do well in school. Writing in the spring of 1979, Professor Shoichi Watanabe of Tokyo's Sophia University called the number of hours that Japanese children are forced to spend each day on studies at school, at home, and at *juku* "a travesty of the spirit of the Child Welfare Law. The situation Japanese children face today is worse even than that of the British children forced to work in coal mines in the days of the Industrial Revolution... What is more, Japanese teachers usually are resentful when their students take supplementary lessons outside the school — an attitude probably unknown elsewhere in the world... The school is jealous of third parties meddling with its children's education; it wants a monopoly on instruction. Rather than endeavoring to help children realize their dreams for the future, the school is preoccupied with keeping its doors closed tight to external influence." Professor Watanabe spoke of "the bitterness of educational servitude, a sentence from which no child can escape," and argued for a voluntary educational system. Despite occasional appeals from people like Professor Watanabe, Japanese students still look like conscripts in a vast educational sea of compulsory 1872-style uniforms — black navy tunics for boys, black navy jumpers for girls.

Professor Watanabe quoted the British historian William Lecky, who said, "A happy youth is in itself an end." He deplored the Japanese system of educational uniformity regardless of aptitude, a system that brings so much unhappiness to so many young people in a country "...where an inordinately high level of homogeneity tends to drive people into bitter competition."

6.   While Japan's inflation rate has been far below that of most countries, including the United States, food prices in Japan are high, largely for political reasons. Since World War II, one political party, the L.D.P. (Liberal Democratic Party) has held power almost constantly. Although Japan is now less than thirty percent rural there has been no electoral redistricting since the end of the war, when the population was seventy percent rural. The rural population is overrepresented by three to one, and the L.D.P. keeps Japan's farm vote loyal by subsidizing farmers even though those farmers are extremely inefficient. The average U.S. farm today is four hundred and fifty acres; the average Japanese farm is 2.9 acres. Food is no longer the bargain it once was in America, yet the average American still pays less than sixteen percent of her/his disposable income on food. The average Japanese spends more than twenty-two percent of disposable income on food.

The Japanese government subsidizes farmers to the extent of about twenty billion dollars per year. The farmers produce more rice than the country consumes (there is little export market for the short-grain rice that the Japanese prefer, especially since the subsidized price is so high that it could sell only with the help of an export subsidy), and the government does little to discourage them. Where does the government get the money to pay the subsidies? It sells imported wheat to Japanese millers at far more than the world price. Even with the profit thus obtained, some tax money is necessary. The result is that roads and housing are short-changed as the farmers continue to grow rice that will never be eaten and as the Japanese continue to pay more than they should for food. American critics of Japanese trade policies say that America could deliver milled flour, rice, beef, frozen juice, and other foods, especially processed foods, to Japan at one fifth the price of the Japanese-produced food. This would not do much to change the imbalance in U.S.-Japanese trade, but it would certainly make life less expensive for Japanese homemakers who are now at the mercy of an obsolete political apportionment system that keeps Japan's rural minority happy at the expense of the urban majority.

7. For centuries the Japanese kept their population stabilized through the practice of *mabiki* — "weeding out" children, especially girls, at birth. Abortion has been legal since the "Eugenic Protection" law was passed in 1948. Japan's population was below eighty million then, but with people returning from China, Korea, and Manchuria, overpopulation was becoming a problem. Today, with the population at one hundred and seventeen million, Japanese women are bearing children at an average rate of 1.74 each. The 1980 birthrate of 13.66 per thousand population was the lowest in Japanese history, even lower than in 1966, when it fell to fourteen per thousand in the Year of the Fiery Horse. It was said that girls born in that year would destroy their husbands, so many women had abortions or otherwise avoided giving birth that year lest they have daughters who might be unmarriagable. (The birthrate climbed back to 19.3 per thousand the following year.)

The birthrate had actually begun to decline after 1964. Up until then, Japanese economic growth had been going straight up. But the economy began to slow in the mid-1960s. More women started to work, and the housing situation began to tighten. It was was also becoming more expensive to raise children. A steep decline in the economy after the 1973 "oil shock" raised prices and was a major factor in reducing the birthrate. Experts say that an average of 2.1 children per family is required to maintain the population at its present level. While some people find the 1.74 rate cheering, and point out that militarists in the 1930s used overpopulation as an excuse for their adventures in Manchuria and China, others (including obstetricians and businessmen with interests in baby bottles, diapers, school satchels, and the like) argue that the Japanese will disappear in another eight centuries or so if they do not increase their birthrate.

A 1979 survey by the *Mainichi Shimbun* showed that the high cost of education was the reason most people gave for not wanting to have more children. The fact that fewer people felt that they could depend upon their children for support in old age was also cited. Of the families surveyed, 20.4 percent had one child, fifty-five percent had two children, 20.1 percent had three children, and 3.5 percent had four or more. Among the fifty-five percent who had two children, 76.6 percent said they did not want any more children; among the 20.4 percent who had only one, 31.1 percent said they did not want any more children. Asked if they practiced birth control, 55.2 percent responded affirmatively. Of those who did not practice birth control, 59.7 percent said they wanted children, 23.1 percent said there were physical factors that prevented them from having children, and 10.2 percent said birth control was unnatural and immoral. Asked about "the Pill," only 78.4 percent of respondents had ever heard of it, and only 3.1 percent said they would use it. The Japanese government has not given official approval to "the Pill," and even among women from twenty to twenty-four, oral contraceptives rank only fourth as the preferred form of birth control despite evidence that for women of that age "the Pill" has almost no risks of undesirable side-effects. The condom is the leading method of birth control employed by women aged twenty to twenty-four (ninety-four percent) and by Japanese women as a whole (81.5 percent), according to the *Mainichi Shimbun* survey. Nearly one-fourth of those interviewed (23.2 percent) relied on the rhythm method, which is one reason for Japan's high abortion rate. Eight percent of the respondents used intrauterine devices (I.U.D.s), and ten percent used other methods, including the diaphragm. Asked why they practiced birth control, 47.3 percent gave reasons involving the health of the mother, possibly a reflection of the fact that so many Japanese women now work; 38.2 percent said it was now too expensive to provide a good education for children; 20.5 percent cited other financial factors, and 16.2 percent said they wanted to live good lives and that having too many children would not permit this. Asked if they had ever had an abortion, 35.4 percent said that they had, and 69.6 percent had had more than one. One out of three abortions involved first pregnancies before or after marriage.

Abortion is permitted under the law only where continued pregnancy or childbirth would be physically harmful to a woman, but that provision of the law is easily evaded (It was once common for American women to come to Japan for abortions). Women have abortions under assumed names, and there have been reports of junior high school girls in major cities collecting money for friends who needed abortions. Japanese law permits "the Pill" to be sold only by prescription, and in recent years various women's groups have demanded the right to buy "the Pill" without a prescription.

When the Keio University Economics Department surveyed three thousand young women in 1972 and asked them how many children they wanted, 60 percent said they wanted three or more. Fewer than three out of ten said they wanted only two children. That was before the "oil shock." A 1981 Keio University survey (the Japanese adore surveys) found that six out of ten wanted only two children. Professor Masaki Yasukawa, who directed the 1981 survey, is a member of the government's Population Problems Advisory Council. He said that wanting two children was not enough to raise the birthrate to the 2.1 replacement level since some women did not, or could not, have children. Allowing for a certain number of infant deaths, he said, more women would have to have three children in order for the two per woman average to be attained. The Ministry of Health and Welfare estimated in 1976 that Japan's population would peak at one hundred and forty million in about 2050 and would remain at that level. Professor Yasukawa had a different prediction: the population, he said, would probably peak at less than one hundred and thirty million in about 2005 and would then begin to decline. Historically, such predictions have been notable in every country for their inaccuracy.

8. To say that Japan's one hundred and seventeen million people are crammed into an area the size of Montana does not begin to suggest the circumstances of life in what I have come to think of as "the crowded crysanthemum." The congestion is at times unbelievable for a Westerner, even one who has braved rush-hour crowds on New York City subways. Most of the population is concentrated in large and medium-sized cities, and that such large numbers of people can be moved to work and back home again each day is a triumph of logistics possible only because Japan's transportation network remains extraordinarily efficient and Japanese commuters are almost invariably patient and polite, if possibly a little masochistic. There are frequent reports of odd items (false teeth, wigs, and the like) being found in trains after their tightly packed human cargoes have been disgorged. Reports of men employed to push passengers into the cars are slightly exaggerated. The young men are at only a few Tokyo stations, notably Shinjuku, and their work is limited to a period of no more than half an hour in the morning when the rush is at its peak.

Despite the overcrowding, Japan is generally considered a desirable country in which to live. The Overseas Development Council, based in Washington, D.C., prepared a Physical Quality of Life Index that was published in November 1981 by the Environmental Fund. On a scale of one to one hundred, the Index rated Sweden at ninety-seven, with Japan, Denmark, Iceland, and the Netherlands close behind at ninety-six. Canada and Switzerland were rated at ninety-five, the United States, the United Kingdom, France, Finland, and New Zealand at ninety-four. Rated at ninety-three were Australia, Austria, Belgium, Czechoslovakia, East Germany, West Germany, and Ireland. Italy and Luxembourg rated ninety-two. The Soviet Union, Poland, Bulgaria, Hungary, and Spain rated ninety-one. Ethiopia and Guinea rated twenty, Somalia nineteen, Afghanistan eighteen, Angola sixteen, Mali fifteen, and Niger only thirteen.

9. The popular name for Tokyo Imperial University, established in 1877 and still officially so called even though Japan is no longer an empire. Todai is actually an abbreviation of Tokyo Daigaku; the last word is Japanese for university as well as for teaching. This university has fourteen thousand students.

10.   According to a 1979 report from the Education Ministry, only 11.1 percent of suicides among junior high school students were related to poor scholastic achievement. About twenty-two percent of the suicidal children were concerned about family affairs, about ten percent were just tired of life, about five percent were worried about their futures, and three percent had mental problems. (I know that does not add up to one hundred percent but this is often the case with the reporting of Japanese statistics. Sloppy journalism is usually responsible, not faulty research.) Among senior high school students, poor scholastic achievement was the biggest reason, according to the report, but it did not give a percentage. Mental troubles accounted for more than twelve percent, family troubles nearly eleven percent, weariness with life 9.2 percent, and concern about their futures 7.3 percent. It should be noted that parents have been known to commit suicide because their sons failed to pass the entrance examination to a prestige university.

Japan's suicide rate is about fifteen per hundred thousand, as compared to eleven per hundred thousand in the United States. Some other countries, including Hungary, Austria, West Germany, Denmark, and Sweden, have higher suicide rates than Japan, despite the fact that Western society takes a dim view of suicide. There is no dishonor in much of Asia, including Japan, in taking one's own life for reasons of sacrifice, renunciation, or apology. Ritual *hara-kiri* is an ancient tradition. A Japanese student who fails a college entrance exam for the second or third time, after having studied night and day for a year between each attempt, may well choose to exit the world this way; so may lovers who have been denied parental permission to marry, men who have failed in business, young men who wish to expiate the debts and sins of their fathers, young widows who are having trouble raising their children. As for suicides among students, Japan does have the dubious distinction of being number one. The teen-age suicide rate is 17.6 per one hundred thousand as compared to 10.9 in the United States, and the incidence of suicides is greatest in the fifteen to twenty-four age group.

The Japanese word for ritual suicide is *seppuku*. The term *hara-kiri* means, literally, to cut (*kiri*) the stomach (*hara*) but only fanatics still commit suicide that way. Most Japanese suicides among juveniles nineteen and under are by hanging. Gas is a distant second,

150

jumping from a high place is third, jumping in front of a moving train is fourth, touching a high voltage wire is fifth, poisoning is sixth, drowning seventh, self-immolation eighth, smothering in a plastic bag ninth, slashing wrists or throat tenth. More than half of juvenile suicides are boys.

11.   The Japanese are prodigious savers, putting aside about twenty yen for every hundred yen they take in, as compared to fourteen or fifteen marks saved per hundred by West Germans and only about five to seven cents saved per dollar by Americans. Putting it another way, the Japanese stash thirteen percent of their Gross National Product into personal savings, the West Germans nine percent, and Americans four percent. The relatively low U.S. rate has existed for nearly a century (it edges up slightly during recessions, when people spend a bit less), and many economists say this has a lot to do with the high rate of inflation in the United States. When the federal government borrows to finance budget deficits, it soaks up a tremendous amount of the investment resources generated by the economy and pushes up interest rates more than would be true if personal savings were higher.

Tax incentives encourage personal saving in Japan as in many other countries (only the United States permits an income tax deduction for interest paid on personal debts, thus encouraging buying on credit rather than giving people more incentive to save). The fact that a Japanese employee often receives a major part of his annual remuneration in the form of midyear and yearend bonuses (*see* note 23) is an even more important factor in explaining Japan's high savings rate.

12.   The Japanese had no written language until Chinese ideographs were introduced in the fifth century. (Up to then, Japan had relied upon professional memorizers — *kataribe* — who were trained from childhood to learn by rote the events of Japanese history, complete with names, dates, and places. In fact, the *kataribe* continued for another three hundred years.) Chinese was the language of government and religion, but the prestigious Chinese characters, numbering in the thousands, were cumbersome and used almost exclusively by men. After the middle of the ninth century, at about the same time that the Cyrillic alphabet was developed in Eastern

Europe, the Japanese developed a phonetic syllabary — *hiragana* — to represent the sounds of everyday speech and to represent things distinctly Japanese for which there were no Chinese *kanji* characters. The Buddhist priest Kobo Daishi arranged this forty-eight syllable syllabary in a poetic verse, *Iroha*, without using a single syllable twice. The syllabary was later simplified by the scholar Shimonoseki so that one or two brush strokes did the work of eight or ten. A little later, the Japanese developed another cursive syllabary, even simpler, that would eventually be used for colloquialisms, foreign words, and special emphasis. This was called *katakana*.

Since it was considered ungraceful for a woman to write in *kanji*, Japanese women used these new syllabaries to create the country's first true literature. *The Pillow-Book of Seishonagon*, compiled at the start of the eleventh century, was a pioneer work in the diary genre, and *Genji Monogatari* (*The Tale of Genji*) by a Japanese baroness of the same period was a pioneer novel that is still a classic of world literature.

Prompted by Americans after World War II, the Japanese reformed their language after the failure of earlier efforts at reform. In 1947, the National Diet approved a recommendation by the Ministry of Education to limit the number of Chinese characters to eighteen hundred and fifty. This reform has not been entirely successful, and older books contain any of eight thousand different *kanji* characters.

Kanji characters are used in conjunction with *hiragana* and *katakana*, but even a typewriter that employed only the two phonetic syllabaries would have to be able to type about a hundred different characters as compared to the twenty-six roman letters and ten arabic numerals used in English and most other European languages. Some Japanese offices are now equipped with ingenious word processors. Toshiba produced the first one. A *hiragana* character appears on the leading edge of each key for a *romaji* (roman) letter or arabic numeral; a button to the left of the keyboard enables the typist to display a series of Chinese *kanji* characters and select the one whose phonetic sound has been indicated by typing the *hiragana* character(s). The printer used by such a word processor must employ something other than the printwheel used by Western word processors. The solution involves a laser beam, or so I am told.

Japanese books open at what Westerners call the "back," and the columns of type are usually vertical. The reader reads from top to bottom and, as with Arabic and Hebrew, from right to left. *Hiragana* characters, derived from vertically written Chinese characters, are connected vertically, are easier to write vertically, and look better when arranged vertically, yet horizontal writing of Japanese began to spread after the start of the Meiji Period (*see* note 36), reflecting the impact of Western horizontal writing. Horizontal writing became even more common in Japan after World War II, with official documents being written horizontally and from left to right. The People's Republic of China has simplified Chinese characters in recent years and has changed to horizontal printing of books and newspapers. This is reportedly true as well in North Korea, but not in South Korea. The Tuareg of the Sahara speak a language called Tamashek, which is basically vertical in written form. As with so many other things in Japan (Shinto wedding ceremonies, Buddhist funerals; Western clothing, kimono; *tatami* mats, carpets; metal tableware, *hashi*), the horizontal and vertical peacefully co-exist. Most Japanese still write their letters vertically, and the demand for vertically arranged diaries is said to be greater than for those horizontally arranged.

13.   Japan has roughly one policeman for every seven hundred and twenty-nine inhabitants; the United States has one for every five hundred and two; France has one for every three hundred and forty seven. A Japanese policeman is given more training and more discretion than law enforcement officers in most countries but he is not authorized to search a suspicious person for weapons. If he uses force in apprehending a suspect he risks prosecution for attempted murder, false arrest, or inflicting bodily injury, and some organized groups are always on the lookout for chances to harrass the police by bringing such charges. There is no law against statutory rape (although forcible violation of a girl under age thirteen is a crime), no law against incest, and no extradition treaty with any country other than the United States. Yet for all the restrictions placed on them, Japan's police have an arrest rate for all crimes of fifty-one percent, as compared with twenty-five percent in the United States and thirty-five percent in Britain. In cases of robbery, the Japanese arrest rate is eighty-three percent, versus thirty-eight percent in the United States, and for murder it is ninety-eight percent, versus ninety-one percent in the United States.

Tokyo, whose population is about 8.5 million (the much larger figures often given include the city's environs), had one hundred and eighty murders in 1980 (New York had twelve times as many, and fourteen times as many rapes), but in the twenty-three central wards of the city there was only one case of a burglar breaking and entering a house and killing someone inside. There was not a single murder during a robbery attempt on the streets, in the parks, or in the subways. Almost all the murders involved family quarrels, and the killers were found in ninety-three percent of the cases.

The Tokyo police force of 44,238 people includes thirteen hundred policewomen and thirty-one hundred and sixty-two non-uniformed office workers. Unlike metropolitan police in American cities, who move about mostly in squad cars, Tokyo's police operate mostly on foot or on bicycles. A policeman is usually called an *omawarisan*, the one who makes his rounds, and each neighborhood has a *koban*, or police box. Someone from the *koban* visits each home in the precinct each year, checking the names, ages, and occupations of its inhabitants. It is common for a policeman to express congratulations upon the birth of a baby and to extend condolences upon a death in the family, creating a dialogue with the community.

Beginning in 1925, when the Japanese had a paranoia about Communists like that in Europe and America, the police were given extraordinary powers that were strengthened early in 1941 under the fascist regime then in power. Some Japanese learned to dread the secret police (*kempetai*) of the military government. Since World War II, the image of Japan's police has changed completely from one of brutality to one of almost benign fairness. Generally, the Japanese willingly cooperate with the local policeman on the beat who, in turn, is inclined to be slightly tolerant of prostitution, homosexual activities, gambling, and other victimless criminal activity to which police in some other countries devote considerable time.

Geographical factors such as the lack of land borders across which a criminal could escape, the common language, a traditional respect for authority, and family pride and honor probably have as much to do with Japan's low crime rate as the effectiveness of the country's well-trained and highly disciplined police. Peer pressure is a strong deterrent to misbehavior in a country where virtually everyone belongs to a group and where there is relatively little alienation of individuals from society, although nearly half of all

Japanese criminal offenders are juveniles which suggests a growing alienation among young people. It should also be noted that Japan has strict handgun control laws and by American standards, virtually no problem of drug abuse. In 1970 there were just over a thousand narcotics offense cases; in 1980 there were about fifteen hundred. Only one company, Dainippon Pharmaceutical, has a license to produce drugs susceptible to abuse, and distribution of the drugs to hospitals is rigidly controlled.

Japanese gangs (*yakuza*) engage in certain illegal activities yet maintain open and friendly relations with the police, who move to curb the *yakuza* only when their activities are considered dangerous to public order. Members of this gangster underworld tend to identify themselves by wearing pinstriped zoot suits with bright red shirts, loud neckties, and dark glasses. There is a Japanese crime syndicate, the *Boryokudan*, which is highly organized and disciplined, although some of its members do carry illegal arms and engage in occasional shootouts with rival organizations. The gangs control the entertainment sections of major cities and their members often act as plainclothes police in those sections, operating under an unwritten code that drunks are not to be robbed or molested. It was once a point of honor with the *Boryokudan* that it would not traffic in hard drugs or even marijuana. Convictions for possession of marijuana or other drugs are rare in Japan and carry stiff criminal penalties. Paul McCartney, the onetime Beatle, narrowly avoided serving a prison term a few years ago by a paying a fine rumored to be the equivalent of half a million dollars.

Most Japanese criminal cases are tried in courts over which three judges preside at the same time, not before juries. When Japan experimented with trial by jury from 1928 to 1943, the accused were given the right to choose between jury trial and the traditional trial by judges. In those fifteen years, only thirty people per year, on average, chose trial by jury. As Professor Ezra Vogel of Harvard noted in his 1979 book *Japan as Number One*, Japan has only about ten thousand lawyers as compared with some three hundred and forty thousand in the United States. American prisons and other correctional institutions had three hundred and forty thousand inmates in 1972, whereas comparable Japanese institutions had only forty thousand. Again quoting Vogel, forty-five percent of the individuals convicted in the United States were sent to prison in 1973, forty-one percent were given probation, and six percent were fined; in Japan the courts fined about ninety-five percent of those found guilty and sent less than five percent to prison. Japan still has capital punishment, yet life imprisonment is considered too cruel and is extremely rare. In cases that do not require a clear decision of guilty or innocent, as in the case of an automobile accident, judges typically have both sides talk the matter out. If one side is repentant, he wins points; if he is arrogant, he loses points. The judges often consider the ability to pay, and if a defendant has an old grandmother who looks as if she had spent her life in the rice fields, this may incline a judge to be sympathetic. Cases are often settled on a seventy-thirty or eighty-twenty basis where an American prosecutor would demand one hundred percent or nothing.

It has been said that Japanese go to court only as a last resort because the community values harmony, because there is a consensus on fundamental principles, because the top man in a corporation can turn away wrath by accepting moral responsibility. More likely, as Professor William Kelly of Yale has written, the reluctance to litigate can be ascribed to the fact that all Japanese lawyers, judges, and prosecutors must be graduates of a two-year program of postgraduate legal education given by the National Legal Training Research Institute. This training insures high uniform standards, but the annual class is limited to five hundred — less than two percent of applicants. Having so few qualified professionals limits expansion of the court system and of legal services to citizens. The average caseload of a Japanese district court judge is five times that of an American district court judge. A Japanese judge, moreover, has no contempt powers and no effective channels of court ordered mediation. The simplest civil case at the district court level can take a whole year, and average disposition time, from filing to decision, is over two years. To pursue a civil suit to judicial conclusion requires great perseverance and can be extremely costly.

14.   Few Japanese single dwellings are equipped with central heating, and this is true even of apartment houses. Central heating was rare in Great Britain as recently as 1965, when only 15 percent of the houses were centrally heated. Today about 60 percent of British houses are centrally heated, but in Japan the percentage remains lower than it was in Britain in 1965. The floor of the Japanese living

room generally has a sunken area, the *kotatsu*, that contains a table covered by a heat-holding quilt; beneath the table is a stove, or *hibachi*, which is generally electric except in some rural areas. The idea is to heat the individual rather than all the interior space, and although it is not always comfortable it does conserve energy.

While most modern housing includes flush toilets, nearly half of all single-family houses more than twenty years old still have nonflush privies set in the floor. In fact, about three percent of new houses built in Tokyo are still equipped with old-fashioned non-flush toilets, set by tradition on the north side of the house, away from the warming sunlight. Trucks with vacuum hoses periodically empty the human waste that collects in household privies and the waste material is then sometimes processed for use as fertilizer. Only about one Japanese house in four has a flush toilet connected with a modern sewage system as compared to more than ninety percent in the United States and an even higher percentage in some other countries. It is common to encounter the sulphurous smell of a leaking septic tank even in chic sections of downtown Tokyo or Osaka. To an American, a smelly privy is unsanitary; to a Japanese, it is unsanitary to sit on a toilet seat that has been used by others, and while some hotels and department stores provide Western-style toilets with seats elevated for comfortable sitting, the Japanese prefer to squat.

15.   A *nakaudo* is the couple which serves as a go-between in the marriage of two persons in Japan. Even where marriages are not arranged, it is customary to have a *nakaudo*, usually a man in a higher position in an organization than the groom, who in company with his wife presents the groom's engagement gift to the bride. According to surveys by the Ministry of Health and Welfare, arranged marriages are on the wane in Japan as more young people find partners on their own. In 1966, 49.8 percent of all marriages were still through *omiai*, which is not an arranged match but an arranged meeting. By 1973, only 36.2 percent were through *omiai*. The Japanese use the word *urenokori*, meaning unsold, for an old maid and consider a woman of twenty-four or twenty-five at great risk of passing the suitable age for marriage (*kekkontekireiki*). In years past, the end of *kekkontekireiki* came at an earlier age. In 1920, the average age at marriage for Japanese women was twenty-two; by

1981, the average was twenty-four. On average, American men and women marry about three years earlier than Japanese, and late marriage is a factor in keeping Japan's birth rate low.

As she gets older, a woman's parents often try to arrange a marriage before it is too late and may accept a less suitable husband than they would have done earlier. Even in the case of younger and perhaps more desirable young women, relatives exchange information about young men (how old is he? what kind of job does he have? what company is he with? what does his father do? how old are his parents? is he the oldest boy in the family? how many brothers and sisters does he have?) to facilitate the matchmaking process. Years ago, it was common for *miaishashin* (matchmaking photographs) to be exchanged. The daughter would be sent to a beauty shop, dressed in her best kimono, and sent to a photographer's studio, but the *miaishashin* was often so heavily retouched that the picture bore little resemblance to the subject. Ordinary *shashin* (snapshots) are now usually exchanged.

If the "grapevine" yields no suitable prospects, a lonely woman (or man) may consult a government matchmaking service. The city of Tokyo has a municipal office, the *koritsu kekkon sodansho*, or public marriage broker, open every day except Monday from nine-thirty to six o'clock and until noon Sunday. An applicant must bring in a birth registration showing parentage and place of birth; a registration showing present place of residence; a photograph slightly larger than passport size; a diploma or degree as evidence of high school, junior college, or college education; a certificate or letter from the applicant's company showing what job the applicant has and what his or her income is; and the applicant's signature stamp. The *koritsu kekkon sodansho* charges nothing for its services, even if it makes a match. In addition, Tokyo's borough government community center provides a free matchmaking service, the *bunkyo-kuyakusho sodansho*, which accepts applicants not only from the city but also from residents of the neighboring Chiba, Kanagawa, and Saitama Prefectures. Three times a year, the *bunkyo-kuyakusho sodansho* holds a *shudanmiai*, or group meeting. People who would like to attend a *shudanmiai* must come to the *bunkyo-kuyakusho sodansho* office at ten o'clock on a Tuesday or Thursday morning with papers similar to those required by the *koritsu kekkon sodansho*. The office claims to bring thirty to forty couples together each year.

Less reputable but obviously popular (the yellow pages in the Tokyo telephone directory list well over one hundred) are the commercial marriage brokers, or *kekkon sodansho*. One of these calls itself the Absolute Elite and claims to have thirty thousand "high class" members, aged twenty to seventy. Absolute Elite hires a first class hotel meeting room twice each month for *shudanmiai* (group meetings) and claims that these have resulted in many successful marriages. Its display advertisement in the yellow pages of the Tokyo classified telephone directory says, "In your life, it is nice to have a beloved partner by your side. That is the only way to find happiness and satisfaction." Most Japanese would seem to agree with that sentiment, but commercial *kekkon sodansho* are less particular than government marriage brokers about credentials, and there is reason to believe that some of the men patronizing their services have something other than marriage on their minds. Some, indeed, may already have wives, and so long as they pay their membership fees, the *kekkon sodansho* does not ask any questions (which may lead to some broken hearts).

One *kekkon sodansho* in Tokyo claims to have two hundred branches from Hokkaido to Kyushu and to match five thousand couples per year. *Zenkoku Nakaudo Rengokai* (National Marriage Broker Association), as it is called, says that it arranges marriages with an on-line computer system, and that it will provide wedding reception facilities, a wedding dress, and so forth upon request. *Ariakekai, another Tokyo kekkon sodansho,* gives an *omiai* party every month, organizes groups for hiking, dancing, and restaurant parties, accepts applicants of any age, and advertises that it arranges second marriages as well as first. Akasaka Elite also has no age limit and promises to arrange both first and second marriages. Akasaka, says the advertisement, is a center for major Japanese companies and the *kekkon sodansho* claims to include lawyers and physicians among its members. (New York City classified telephone directories once carried quite a few marriage broker advertisements, most of them for *shadchen* serving the immigrant Jewish community. Today's Manhattan directory lists some computer dating services but only two matrimonial broker services.)

More common and more respectable in Japan, it is the *nakaudo* who sets up the *omiai*, or meeting. This may be at the *nakaudo's* home, at the home of the son or daughter's parents, or at a restaurant or coffee shop. (The Kabuki Theater was once a common meeting place.) The daughter may appear only briefly, perhaps to serve tea if the *omiai* is at her parent's house, but at least the young man and woman get an opportunity to see each other, which was not the case in the past. Only since World War II have young men and women who met at an *omiai* proceeded to go out on dates together before deciding whether or not they wanted to marry. Today, if they want to get married, or call off the relationship, they still tell the *nakaudo*, and parents may still tell the *nakaudo* that they want the relationship broken off, although that is no longer common. Many girls today do not want to marry oldest sons because it means that they will have to take care of the husband's parents. The idea of an arranged marriage is foreign to most Westerners, but a Japanese woman wrote a few years ago that she had told two Frenchwomen — sisters who were over twenty-five — about the practice and had found them envious.

While the typical Japanese man is by no means uxorious, the Japanese are probably the most marrying people in the world. By age twenty-six, ninety-seven percent of Japanese women have been married, although some may have lost their husbands or be divorced. Unmarried men and women are looked upon with suspicion, and a company may think that an unmarried man is immature and a social misfit whose chances for advancement are diminished. Japanese women complain about the lack of job opportunities, but most still dream of having good marriages. According to a book published in September 1979, the counselor at an Osaka high school asked girls in her district to write essays on the subject, "What is Woman's Happiness?" For seventy percent of the girls, happiness was being married and having cute babies. To be a good wife and mother might be ordinary, the girls said, but it was the best way to be happy.

16.   An *oseibo* is a yearend gift originally intended as a gesture to repay an individual for personal obligations piled up in the course of the year. Gifts made at midyear are called *ochugen*. Today the gift may be given with the purpose of currying favor with a superior in hopes of protecting a man's position in the company's hierarchy and perhaps smoothing the path toward a promotion, annual prom-

otions being made shortly after New Year's. Ambitious company men agonize about giving too little or too much and thus offending a higher-up. Age forty is a critical one for promotion and a man who might have thought some years earlier that giving *oseibo* was a stupid custom often has a different attitude as he approaches that age. Many Japanese companies have tried to stop the intra-office system of paying tribute with *oseibo*; few have had much success. Companies that spent well over three trillion yen (actually about $15.75 billion) on tax-deductible entertainment in 1980 pay enormous sums of money each year on fancy gift packages of dried seaweed, green tea, canned ham, imported whisky, neckties, designer jewelry, and the like for major clients, customers, and government bureaucrats with whom they must deal on a regular basis. This useof gifts to grease the wheels of personal and business relationships is so accepted in Japan that the *oseibo* is not about to disappear. The government has insisted in recent years that public officials return gifts from foreign officials or politicians if the gifts are worth the equivalent of one hundred dollars or more, or that they turn the gifts over to the proper authorities. There is some doubt as to how seriously this order is taken.

Few, if any, books about modern Japanese society make any mention of Thorstein Veblen, the University of Chicago social scientist whose 1899 classic *The Theory of the Leisure Class* might almost have been written with today's Japan in mind. Not that Japan has ever had much of a leisure class; neither did the United States in 1899 nor even today. Veblen's point was that societies behave in certain ways and adopt certain tastes as evidence of gentility since the customs and tastes can be acquired only with leisure. Drunkenness, still quite acceptable in Japan, could be called "conspicuous leisure" (*see* note 24). Rich Chinese girls (*not* Japanese) for centuries had their feet bound so that they would be conspicuously unable to walk when they grew up; while this is an extreme example, it illustrates the point that people will go to great lengths to show that they — or at least the women in the family — do not have to work. Veblen would have called it "conspicuous leisure," or perhaps "vicarious leisure," since the father of the girl may have to work for a living but wants enforced idleness for his wife and child to enhance his prestige. A man wearing "stainless linen, [a] lustrous cylindrical hat, and [carrying a] walking stick" was showing the world that he did not have to toil with his hands, Veblen said, and he called these items insignia of "conspicuous leisure." Ladies of leisure in his day wore corsets and high heels, which rendered their wearers "infirm," as Veblen put it. The widespread reluctance of Japanese husbands to let their wives work is a present-day example of "vicarious leisure." So is the resistance to hiring women with four-year university degrees. When Veblen was writing at the end of the nineteenth century, few American or European women went to college. "It is felt," said Veblen, "that women should, in all propriety, acquire only such knowledge as may be classed under one or the other of two heads: [1] such knowledge as conduces immediately to a better performance of domestic service the domestic sphere; [2] such accomplishments and dexterity, quasi-scholarly and quasi-artistic, as plainly comes in under the head of performance of vicarious leisure. Knowledge is felt to be unfeminine if it is knowledge which expresses the unfolding of the learner's own life, the acquisition of which proceeds on the learner's own cognitive interest, without prompting from the canons of propriety, and without reference back to a master whose comfort or good repute is to be enhanced by the employment or the exhibition of it. So, also, all knowledge which is useful as evidence of leisure, other than vicarious leisure, is scarcely feminine." (The education of Raicho Hiratsuka's mother described in note 1 may be instructive in illustrating Veblen's point.)

Veblen also introduced such concepts as "conspicuous consumption" and "conspicuous waste." Where it was not practical for either a husband or wife to be conspicuously idle, he said, then at least the wife and children could be conspicuous in their consumption of goods. "Not even the most abjectly poor (class of society) forgoes all customary conspicuous consumption. The last items of this category of consumption are not given up except under stress of the direst necessity," he maintained. "Very much of squalor and discomfort will be endured before the last trinket or the last pretense of pecuniary decency is put away," said Veblen, and one has only to look at a street beggar smoking cigarettes to see evidence of conspicuous consumption — a person "burning money," as it were.

Both these exercises in vanity — conspicuous consumption and conspicuous waste — are rampant in modern Japanese society, where everyone seems bent on making what the Italians call a *bella figura*. Veblen would, in fact, have ascribed Japan's low birthrate (*see* note 7) in large part to the demands of conspicuous waste. Remembering that ninety percent of the Japanese are middle class, or at least think of themselves as being middle class, consider this statement by Veblen: "The low birthrate of the classes upon whom the requirements of reputable expenditure fall with great urgency is likewise traceable to the exigencies of a standard of living based on conspicuous waste. The conspicuous consumption, and the consequent increased expense, required in the reputable maintenance of a child is very considerable and acts as a powerful deterrent. It is probably the most effectual of the Malthusian prudential checks."

Japanese hotel lobbies are often grandly spacious to the point of making the public rooms of Western hotels, built on less costly land, look positively cramped. The passion for golf in a country without much space for golf courses, a passion that can usually be indulged only by paying an astronomic sum for country club membership [although driving ranges are seen everywhere] is another illustration of "conspicuous consumption" or "conspicuous waste." So is the national obsession with gift-giving. Few Japanese would think of making a business or social call without an appropriate *omiyage* (gift), and what appears to be an innocuous souvenir shop in an arcade will not uncommonly display neckties priced at twenty thousand yen (about one hundred dollars) for the visitor who needs an impressive last minute *omiyage*.

Gift-giving is obligatory in Japan. When you receive your yearend or midyear bonus, you give *oseibo* or *ochugen*. When you are married, you receive *oiwai* (often money gifts intended to help defray the considerable costs of a Japanese wedding), and you also bestow gifts upon the wedding guests. (Many foreigners are shocked when a maid informs them that they are expected to spend substantial sums of money to reciprocate for wedding gifts.) In case of a death in the family, friends of the family present *koden* (gifts of sympathy), and the mourners present gifts in return. A gift, incidentally, is never opened in the presence of the giver: bad manners.

17. I had suggested that it was because the Japanese spend so many hours commuting to work by train, often packed into cars so closely that holding a newspaper is almost impossible.

18. No other country publishes so many book titles every year as the United States. According to a United Nations survey, there were 85,287 titles published in the United States in 1977, 78,697 in the Soviet Union, 40,616 in West Germany, 35,526 in the United Kingdom, 34,590 in Japan, 28,245 in France, 23,527 in Spain, 12,706 in India, 12,028 in the Netherlands, and 11,239 in Yugoslavia.

19. Japanese students go to school two hundred and forty days out of the year, Saturday mornings included, as do many European students. American students average one hundred and eighty days.

20. The yearend bonus, generally three months' pay and sometimes twice that, is not based on an individual's performance but rather on the company's performance. Each employee receives a fraction of his or her salary, and that fraction is the same for each. In a bad year, a company may defer payment of the midyear or yearend bonus — or even both — to a later year, thus in effect cutting its payroll by as much as twenty-five to thirty-five percent without laying off any employee. This flexibility is perhaps the primary reason that large Japanese companies are able to guarantee lifetime employment and can have loyal, experienced workers who co-operate to make their companies successful rather than concentrating their efforts on outstanding individual accomplishment as in Western companies. Receiving pay in large lump sums under the bonus system also helps to explain Japan's high rate of savings (*see* note 11).

21. Rice provides about half the average Japanese caloric intake; *mochi* are rice cakes traditionally consumed to celebrate the new year. Made from a paste of pounded steamed rice, these dumpling-like creations are eaten in soup or served baked. They are especially indigestible, and deaths occur each year among children and older people who have choked on *mochi* or whose intestinal tracts have been unequal to the demands of these potentially deadly rice cakes.

22. The grounds of Tokyo's Meiji Shrine occupy about one hundred and seventy-five acres of land in Yoyogi, Shibuya-ku, that was often visited by the Emperor Meiji, who reigned from 1868 until his death in 1912, and his consort the Empress Shoken, who died in 1914. (The Meiji era marked the end of the Tokugawa shogunate that had ruled Japan since 1600. Both the emperor and empress were worshipped as deities.) The shrine itself is made of the best Japanese cypress wood from Kiso, a stone building to the north houses a display of articles used by the imperial couple, and Shinto wedding ceremonies are often performed in a memorial hall located in a corner of the Meiji Jingu Outer Garden, which includes specimens of all the trees and shrubs that grow in Japan.

23. A survey made in the mid-1970s showed that sixty-four percent of Japanese husbands stop off "somewhere" on the way home, and very few tell their wives when they are going to be home late. The popularity of surveys in Japan is related to the great esteem for statistical methods introduced in the 1950s by the American statistician W. E. Deming (*see* note 45).

24. Japanese men do not drink as much as they did when drinking was virtually the only leisure-time activity available to them. It used to be that a man would almost have to go to a bar and drink with his superior after work, and sometimes when a man could not express himself otherwise he would pretend to be drunker than he was and would say something that he could not say while sober; or his superior might get drunk and while in his cups might sadistically burn a junior's hand with his cigarette end, explaining afterward that he had been drunk. Young people today will not accept that kind of behavior, and most would rather have a formal dinner than a big drinking party. Still, there is no opprobrium attached to drunkenness in Japan as there is in Western countries. Some observers ascribe this phenomenon of tolerating drunkenness to what they call a broadminded attitude, but one cannot help remembering what Thorstein Veblen (*see* note 16) said about inebriation. A man who has had too much to drink cannot work, so one might think that Veblen would have called drunkenness a way of expressing "conspicuous leisure" or "conspicuous waste." In fact, he had a

slightly different view, but one whose validity is confirmed when one sees a Japanese wife pouring sake for her husband.

"...The base classes, primarily the women, practice an enforced continence with respect to ... stimulants, except in countries where they are obtainable at a very low cost. From archaic times down through all the length of the pátriarchal regime it has been the office of the women to prepare and administer these luxuries, and it has been the perquisite of the men of gentle birth and breeding to consume them. Drunkenness and the other pathological consequences of the free use of stimulants therefore tend in their turn to become honorific, as being a mark ... of the superior status of those who are able to afford the indulgence. Infirmities induced by over-indulgence are among some peoples freely recognized as manly attributes..."

Sake (pronounced sah-keh), the traditional Japanese drink, is usually warmed to a temperature of one hundred and ten to one hundred and twenty degrees fahrenheit before serving. Generally called rice wine, sake is actually produced by a brewing process closer to beermaking, although its alcoholic content, fifteen to twenty percent, is slightly higher than that of wine or beer. Yokohama's Kirin Brewery was started under the name Spring Valley Brewery by an American, William Copeland, in 1869 and Kirin Beer, along with Asahi and Sapporo, is so good that Japanese beer consumption passed sake consumption in the 1960s. Japan is also a whisky producer; Suntory, Ltd., originally a winery, has been distilling a "Scotch" type whisky since the 1920s.

Given the much greater freedom enjoyed by young Japanese women today, it is common to see women in beer halls, some of them showing the effects of alcohol. That was never seen before the war, yet conservative Japanese are no longer open in the criticism of women drinking, and half the customers in a beer hall are sometimes women.

25.   A survey taken in the mid-1970s asked Japanese men whom they would telephone first if there was an earthquake. Only nine percent said they would phone their wives; thirty-seven percent said they would phone their employers. The Japanese call this devotion to the company *Aisha Seishin*. It has a lot to do with the

success of Japanese companies in competing with companies in the United States and other countries.

26.   A survey by the prime minister's office a few years ago found that twenty-five percent of Japanese women did not really want to get married; they simply felt it was not the road to fulfillment for them. Of the sixty-two percent who did choose to get married, only twelve percent said they expected any happiness out of it (*see* note 15). There is an old Japanese saying: *Kekkon wa josei no hakaba de aru*, meaning "Marriage is a woman's grave."

27.   According to 1980 Ministry of Health and Welfare figures, 70.2 percent of Japanese men over age twenty still smoked. That was a 2.9 percent decline from the 1979 level and may be explained in part by the fact that Japanese cigarette prices went up twenty-one percent in April 1979. (Only 36.7 percent of American men over age twenty still smoked in 1980, according to figures from the National Federation for Health Statistics. Among certain ethnic groups, the percentage was somewhat higher.) Only 14.4 percent of Japanese women over age twenty smoked, a decline of one percent from 1979. (In the United States, *more adult women than men are smokers.* Smoking, in fact, has declined in recent years among all segments of the American population with the exception of teen-age girls; 38.9 percent of American women smoked in 1980 as compared with 36.7 percent of adult men.) While only 15.4 percent of American smokers smoke thirty-five or more cigarettes a day, another 13.2 percent smoked twenty-five to thirty-four a day and 42.4 percent smoked fifteen to twenty-four cigarettes a day. Japanese men who smoked every day (67.4 percent of total male smokers) averaged 24.6 cigarettes (Hope, Peace, and Hi-Lite are some major brands) each day, up slightly from 1979. Japanese women who smoked every day averaged 15.7 cigarettes each day, down slightly from 1979. These figures are based on a mail survey of about sixteen thousand adult men and women in July 1980. The Ministry of Health survey drew a response of eighty-one percent and the figures probably understate the extent of the Japanese addiction to cigarette smoking. Writing in the summer of 1978, the Japanese writer Atsuko Chiba quoted somewhat lower figures, saying that three out of five adult Japanese

males smoked as compared with two out of five adult American males, but she calculated that five thousand cigarettes went up in smoke per square mile in Japan each day as compared with four hundred and sixty per day in the United States. Person for person, she said, the Japanese were the heaviest cigarette users in the world, and although a few activists led by a young woman advertising copywriter, Midori Nakadan, have formed an Association to Protect Nonsmokers, membership is "tiny." (It numbered only twenty-five hundred in the summer of 1978.)

Midori Nakadan's Association has appealed unsuccessfully to the Diet to enact laws against smoking in such places as hospital lobbies. In fact, the government tobacco monopoly has tried, without much success, to increase smoking among women. Atsuko Chiba suggested that one reason women resist is that they have been told that smoking is bad for the complexion. She also suggested that heavy smoking among Japanese men was related to the acute tensions of life and to the fierce competition in Japanese firms, where elaborately polite behavior masked bitter rivalry for promotion. The Japan Tobacco and Salt Corporation, a government monopoly created in 1904 to finance the war against czarist Russia, has voluntarily restricted television, newspaper, and magazine advertising to new brands of cigarettes. It has also directed some efforts that encourage Japanese smokers toward "Smokin' Clean" (a legend that appears in English all over the country) and dispose of their butts properly. Commuters are told not to smoke on subway and railway station platforms during rush hours. Aside from that, the government monopoly does nothing to discourage cigarette use, which produces billions of dollars in revenues for central and local governments. United States congressmen from North Carolina and other tobacco-growing states make it difficult for American authorities to pursue effective programs that would reduce the rate of illness and death related to smoking. Japan, on the other hand, protects her domestic tobacco industry with high agricultural tariffs and allows a profit-making government monopoly to frustrate efforts that might reduce the cigarette death toll.

For people (including many smokers) with an aversion to smoke-filled air, Japan can be a nightmare. Anti-pollution demonstrators march through the city puffing cigarettes, and at public meetings to protest air pollution the air is certain to be filled with cigarette smoke. The famous Japanese National Railways *shinkansen* "bullet trains" generally have only one no-smoking car (Car No. 1 as a rule), and the usually law-abiding Japanese often ignore the no-smoking rule even in that one car. Unless one waits on the platform at the designated place for the no-smoking car at the beginning of the train's run, it may be impossible to obtain a seat in that car.

On JAL (Japan Air Lines) flights, the no-smoking section is usually a token couple of rows in the back of the aircraft. On domestic flights of All-Nippon Airways, the situation is at least as heavily weighted against non-smokers. The Japanese once called Westerners *bata-kusai*, or butter-stinkers, because, as one Japanese wrote, "Westerners have a strong body odor which is quite nauseating. The body odor of the average American or Englishman is undoubtedly the result of a heavy meat diet." Eating animal fat, whether it is butter or the fat in meats, does produce butyric acid, which gives the eater a definite odor that few Westerners notice. Relatively few Japanese seem to notice the stench of cigarette smoke that pervades so many public places in Japan (and on the JAL flights to and from Japan). Consciousness-raising efforts have not been very successful, and it must be said with regard to smoking that Japan, so far ahead of the world in some other ways, suffers from a culture lag.

28.   The Empress Gemmei, who came to power in A.D. 707, made Nara the capital of Japan in 710 and it remained the capital until 794. Before 710, there had been a new capital with each new emperor or empress. In 794, the capital was moved to nearby Kyoto, and in 1868 it was moved to Tokyo. Nara remains an important cultural center with major Buddhist temples and bronze statues, including the fifty-five-foot tall *Rushanabutsu* figure completed in 752. In 1981, after a television fund-raising campaign by a local Buddhist priest, a pagoda was completed at Nara to replace one that had been destroyed by fire centuries earlier. Its twin, completed in the thirteenth century and still standing, was matched in every detail.

29.   A *futon* is a bulky sleeping comforter which is spread on the floor at night, rolled up and stored in a closet or cupboard during the day. Its weight has been listed with some authority as a contributory factor in causing several serious ailments. Fabrics used in the past to

cover *futons* have often been of outstanding beauty. These cotton fabrics, some more than a century old, are today used to create jackets, neckties, handbags, book jackets, and the like. An Osaka shop that specializes in such items is the Free Market at 1-F, Shiba-kawa Building, 4-33 Higashifushimi-cho, Higashi-ku.

30. *Hashi*, or *o-hashi*, are wooden (or sometimes plastic or metal) eating sticks, smaller than the Chinese utensils that Westerners call "chop-sticks." The disposability of *hashi* is related to Shinto principles of cleanliness and constant renewal. The use of wood for eating utensils has been related to the hypersensitive Japanese palate, wood being neutral in taste and not likely to impinge on the taste of what is being eaten. In his 1965 book *The Kimono Mind*, Bernard Rudofsky said that metal forks and spoons might not have any detectible taste to a Westerner, but when a piece of tin foil gets in your mouth while eating cheese, "you may perceive its nauseating sweetness. Yet the taste of tin foil differs from the taste of other metals only in degree." Anyone who has tasted tin foil while eating chocolate will have experienced a similarly unpleasant sensation, but the Japanese use of metal *hashi* (actually more common among Koreans than Japanese) raises questions about the validity of Rudofsky's point.

31. Japanese skin tones are decidedly not yellow. My wife Chie's skin is ruddier than mine and it is hard to know where the idea began that Orientals have "yellow" skin.

32. The name *Itai Itai* came from a physician named Kono who examined patients suffering from painful symptoms in the town of Fuchu-machi in 1955. Out of some twenty-four thousand people living along a stream of the Jintsu River in that town, more than two hundred came down with Dr. Kono's *Itai Itai* disease and thirty-two died. The victims were all women, they were all between the ages of fifty and sixty, and all had borne a good many children. Their symptoms began with rheumatic-like lumbago pains in the back, shoulder, or knee joints. Then their bones became brittle as calcium and other minerals were lost, and many suffered painful fractures, became shortened in height, or experienced kidney damage. The cause of their problem was not identified for several years. A cadmium mining plant upstream from Fuchumachi had been discharging metal wastes into the river, and the river had been depositing

particles of cadmium in rice fields. Cadmium from food and water contaminated with the mineral had accumulated in the bones of the people, yet it had all happened so gradually that nobody knew it. It is still uncertain why older mothers were singled out as victims. In extreme cases of cadmium poisoning, a severe coughing fit is enough to break an entire rib cage. If larger amounts of the metal are ingested, it produces vomiting as the body reacts to protect itself, but tiny amounts work silently and invisibly.

Cadmium poisoning made headlines after Takako Nakamura, a twenty-eight-year-old lathe operator, commited suicide by throwing herself from a speeding train in 1969. Her diary was later found, and the entries included passages such as this one: "The doctors cannot diagnose my disease. I am afraid it is cadmium poisoning. It is running through my whole body. Pain eats away at me. I feel that I want to tear out my stomach. Tear out all my insides and cast them away." The woman's body was exhumed in 1971 and an autopsy revealed that Nakamura had indeed suffered from cadmium poisoning. Cadmium occurs in small amounts in zinc ores, and Nakamura had inhaled cadmium fumes on her job at the Toho Zinc Company. When Prime Minister Eisaku Sato heard about the case, he wept in public and announced that he was determined to secure passage of strong anti-pollution legislation, no matter how much opposition Japanese industry mounted against him.

The owner of a paint factory in Nagano City became so depressed over the cadmium poisoning scandal that he took his life, leaving a farewell note that said, "I would like to stop using cadmium but I cannot. I am assuming full responsibility and choosing death." However, Masu Araki, the chairman of the National Public Safety Commission, made a speech in which he said, "The human body has functions to discharge foreign wastes. We must have the spirit to eat contaminated rice."

The much-publicized Minamata disease of the 1950s got that name because the mercury poisoning, which is what it was, affected residents of Minamata City in Kyushu. More than a hundred people were affected, mostly fishermen and their families. More than fifty died, and scores of others went blind, lost the use of limbs, or suffered brain damage. Minamata disease was found in 1959 to have been caused by diets consisting chiefly of fish and shellfish that had been contaminated with alkyl mercury discharged with waste water over a period of decades by the vinyl chloride plant of the Shin-Nihon Chisso Hiryo Company. In 1965, a similar episode seriously affected seventy people and took seven lives at Niigata, on the northwest coast of Honshu, Japan's main island. The chemical company Showa Denko, it developed, had been dumping industrial wastes into the Agano River, and in the fall of 1971 the company made an out-of-court settlement. The plaintiffs were given eight hundred and ten thousand dollars, just over half what they had demanded. The face-saving settlement was enormous by Japanese standards, incredibly low by American standards.

Japan's Waste Management and Public Cleansing Law, enforced since 1971, has improved the nation's environment, and there is vigorous regulation of pollutants and prosecution of polluters under the Air Pollution and Water Pollution Control Laws. The legislation has been amended several times to keep environmental pollution at a minimum, and Japan has pioneered in making polluters pay compensation costs based on civil liability.

33.   What Sachiko would actually have written, translated phonetically, is "Noebbia." The Japanese have difficulty pronouncing the letters "l" and "v." They also add vowels at the end of words that Westerners end with consonants. "Hotel," for example, is pronounced "hoteru." This does not for a moment discourage Japanese companies from naming themselves, or their products, in ways that are certain to be mispronounced. The Yokohama automobile maker Nissan Motor (which for years called its export cars Datsuns but has been changing that practice) sells models in its domestic market with names like Violet, Laurel, Langley, and Leopard. Toyo Kogyo of Hiroshima, which produces Mazdas, has models named Lancer, Bluebird, and Familia. Neither of these companies to my knowledge sells models in the American market with names containing "v"s and "l"s. Along Japanese highways, one occasionally sees a billboard advertising Lilac chocolates. There is no way that the ordinary Japanese is going to pronounce Violet, Laurel, Langley, Lancer, Bluebird, Familia, or Lilac in a way recognizable to a Westerner, any more than an ordinary American is going to pronounce certain French words and be understood by a native Frenchman. It is not a matter of physical peculiarity, simply

one of cultural difference. A Japanese person *can* learn the Western pronunciation of words contained "l"s and "v"s, but why bother? In discussing cosmetics, people are quite content to use Japanese pronunciations and will chatter happily away about Kurabu (Club) cosmetics, Fruberu (Flouveil) cosmetics, and Noebbia (Noevir) cosmetics, which in some cases may quite deliberately be given exotic, foreign sounding names.

34. Two mail deliveries per day is still the standard in Japan. Women as well as men deliver mail.

35. "Noriko" (the name has been changed) worked in a branch office of Hitachi, the big electrical manufacturing company. A male employee grew very fond of her but was transferred to another branch of the company. When he returned to the office one day to inquire about her, he was told, in error, that she had left the company and that her whereabouts were unknown.

36. From 1185 until 1868, the Japanese emperor was a puppet of the shoguns (generals) who ruled the country through centuries of conflict between *daimyo* (feudal lords). The emperor Mutsuhito ascended the throne in February 1867 but, like all the other emperors since 1185, had no power until the abdication of the last Tokugawa shogun Yoshinobu in November 1867. In April 1868, while Benjamin Disraeli was organizing a new Tory government in Britain and U.S. Senators were trying to impeach President Andrew Johnson, the Japanese emperor signed an oath pledging himself to be guided by an assembly (the Diet) responsive to public opinion. The last Tokugawa forces were defeated at the Battle of Ueno July 4, 1868, and the city of Edo (Ueno was then a neighboring town) was renamed Tokyo, meaning eastern capital, in November. The imperial family took over Edo Castle in the center of town that had been used by shoguns for centuries, and the emperor Mutsuhito became the Meiji emperor.

37. *Samurai* were retainer knights of the *daimyo* (feudal lords) and *shogun* who struggled for power through so much of Japanese history. In 1869, the year after the Meiji restoration, chiefs of Japan's four great clans surrendered their territories to the Meiji emperor;

the Satsuma, Choshu, Tosa, and Hizen *daimyo* were made governors of their former provinces. This left the old *samurai* warrior class with no reason for existence, and the emperor not only denied them pensions but forbade them to wear their traditional two swords. The *samurai* grumbled about the "evil counselors" who had the ear of the young emperor, and in January 1877, when the emperor was still only twenty-five, *samurai* of the Satsuma clan in Japan's southern island of Kyushu began the Satsuma Rebellion. A modern army, funded by a large issue of paper money, crushed the rebellion by September.

38. Prostitution has never had the stigma in Japan that it has had elsewhere in the world. When the Tokugawa shogun Ieyasu died in 1616, his last injunction was that prostitution was necessary if adultery was to be avoided. In order to keep his feudal lords (*daimyo*) from getting too rich and amassing too much power, Ieyasu had enforced a system called *sankinkotaiseido*: the *daimyo* were required to make costly journeys to Edo (the old name for Tokyo) every other year and to remain there for a year with their *samurai*, who had to leave their wives at home. When a *daimyo* returned to his home *ryochi*, or province, he had to leave his wife and children hostage at Edo. Like the *daimyo*, richer *samurai* could afford mistresses; while in Edo, poorer *samurai* had to depend upon the services of prostitutes.

Tokyo's Yoshiwara brothel district was established at Edo in 1617, the year after Ieyasu's death, when a local vice lord persuaded the Tokugawa authorities to grant him a license to operate an area of supervised prostitution. In return, he promised to keep his eye out for suspicious strangers. Given the license, he found an empty field full of reeds (*Yoshiwara* meant reedy field; later, a different character was subsituted for the Yoshi and the name became happy field). The district was moved after a fire in 1656 to the Asakusa section of Edo, and grew to have a street lined with good restaurants, public baths, and expensive shops. The section remained in operation until April 1, 1958, despite efforts by U.S. occupation forces to close it down. Girls were placed in the brothels under long-term contracts beginning as early as age six or seven. At age twelve, if she was able to pass an examination, a girl rose from the status of *kamuro*, or apprentice, to *shinzo*; she was trained in singing, dancing, poetry composition, and lovemaking until she was seventeen, at which time she was given another examination. If she failed, she might never be anything more than a maid; if she passed, she became an *oiran*, the highest level of prostitute, and might in time even achieve the status of *tayu*, the highest of three grades of *oiran*.

In 1649, the year in which England's Charles I was beheaded and in which the Tokugawa government issued its proclamation concerning the duties of farmers' wives (*see* note 2), the shogun saddled farmers with a new tax that requistioned virtually all their rice and obliged them to subsist on millet. The farmers were forced to put their wives to work weaving cloth and to send surplus children to work in the city. Then and in future centuries, a young girl selected to save her family from financial ruin by accepting employment in a brothel was regarded with pity and respect, not scorn. It was a romantic age. The English Cavalier poet Richard Lovelace wrote his poem "To Lucasta, on Going to the War" in 1649: "I could not love thee, dear, so much/ Loved I not honour more." A young Japanese prostitute was not without a certain honor. While she might with rare fortune become the mistress of a rich admirer, it was almost unheard of for anyone to marry such a woman. She could no longer entertain dreams of having a home and family of her own. There was a poignancy about her role that has inspired much Japanese literature.

The word for a Japanese red-light district is *karyukai*, or "flower and willow world." The word for prostitution is *baishun*, a word written with two ideographs; the first can be read *bai* or *uru*, meaning to sell, and the second can be read *shun* or *haru*, meaning the season of spring; so a woman of the flower and willow world was selling spring. It was difficult for a woman who sold spring ever to save enough money to buy out her contract and secure her freedom. A Yoshiwara prostitute did not have much freedom. She was permitted to cross the moat and leave the district only to visit a dying parent or to go with other prostitutes to see the cherry blossoms in Ueno. *Samurai* were not permitted to enter the district but often went in disguise. The gates of the district were closed at the midnight curfew hour, and this city within a city — called the *Fuyajo*, or the castle that knows no night — continued its revels until the gates reopened at six o'clock the next morning.

In 1872, a ship stopped at Yokohama carrying Chinese slaves

bound for Peru. The Japanese government refused to give the ship clearance and insisted that the slaves be returned to China. The captain of the ship replied that the Japanese were also engaged in selling people, citing the houses of prostitution to support his argument. The Meiji government thereupon enacted a law forbidding people to sell their daughters as prostitutes or *geisha* and said that existing prostitutes were free to leave without having to pay for their freedom. According to the law, the women had no rights as human beings, and since horses and cows did not have to repay debts, the women did not have to repay theirs. The *geisha* and prostitutes could not return to their homes, they had no other means of supporting themselves, and the law simply meant more hungry people. Poor farmers had no choice in bad times but to sell their daughters, so the law was made flexible. If a girl wished to become a *geisha* or prostitute, the government might give approval after looking into the case. The practice of selling daughters continued into the Showa period and was prevalent during the Great Depression of the 1930s.

39.   Nearly one hundred thousand demonstrators assembled on the Mall in the nation's capital July 9, 1978, to support an extension of the seven-year deadline for ratification of the Equal Rights Amendment beyond March 22, 1979. Many of the participants were dressed in white like early suffragists, and parallels were drawn to a demonstration led by the American women's rights pioneer Alice Paul, whose five thousand followers were subjected to great abuse when they marched down Pennsylvania Avenue on March 3, 1913. The English women's rights pioneer Emmeline Pankhurst was inciting her supporters at that time to place explosives in the house of the Chancellor of the Exchequer David Lloyd George as part of their campaign to gain the vote for British women and she was sentenced to a prison term. Paul, who was then twenty-seven, founded the National Woman's Party to fight for female suffrage in the United States. Washington city police turned their backs on her march while angry, jeering men spat upon the women, slapped them, and poked them with lighted cigars. Before the women could reach the White House, counter-demonstrators broke up the march at the National Archives building. It took a cavalry troop from Fort Myer to restore order, and forty people were hospitalized. American women did not get voting rights nationwide until August 26, 1920,

when the Tennessee legislature ratified the Nineteenth Amendment in time for the women to help elect handsome (and inept) Warren G. Harding to the presidency. The July 1978 march, held in ninety degree weather on a typically muggy Washington summer afternoon, was the largest feminine gathering in the world and it marked the start of a renewed effort to obtain ratification of the Equal Rights Amendment. Whereas it took little more than fourteen months for the Nineteenth Amendment to be ratified, the Equal Rights Amendment encountered considerable opposition and had still not been ratified by the necessary two-thirds of the states at the time this book went to press. Only three more states were needed at the time of the 1978 march and that number had not changed by the summer of 1982.

40.   Unless some other source is specified, all information in this note comes from the book *Abunai Keshohin* [*Dangerous Cosmetics*], published by the Association of Japanese Consumers in 1979 or from its sequel, published under the same title in 1981. I have disguised company and brand names, some of them American.

In July 1975, the Association of Japanese Consumers, Osaka branch, held a special meeting and organized Cosmetic 110 (110 is the emergency telephone number all over Japan, comparable to 911 in the United States (which began in New York City in 1968) and 999 in Britain (which began in 1937). At least fifty women at the meeting suffered from *kokuhisho*, or black skin syndrome, and it later developed that the syndrome affected some men who had used certain brands of after-shave lotion. Japan's largest cosmetic maker is Shiseido Co., Ltd., which was founded in 1927 but which really began as a Tokyo pharmacy (in the 1890s it introduced the first toothbrushes made in Japan). Shiseido established a consumer consultation office in 1976 to deal with complaints from women who had problems related to using Shiseido products, but the company never admitted to any responsibility for the problems. In July 1977, a group of women brought suit against seven different cosmetic makers in an Osaka court. They asked for combined damages of one hundred and seventy million yen, or about eight hundred and fifty thousand dollars. However, it was difficult for a woman to prove that she used one brand of makeup rather than another, and that a product made by one particular company was clearly to blame for her skin troubles, so the trial dragged on for four and a half years. Six of the women agreed to a settlement of two hundred and fifty thousand dollars before the trial was decided. In 1981, the Osaka court ruled in favor of the women and the cosmetic companies agreed to try their best to prove the safety of their products. In another case, six Tokyo women received the equivalent of one hundred thousand dollars from two cosmetic companies. The public relations director of one large company said that his people had never used Red 219, the coal-tar dye that was blamed for most of the trouble. (The Japanese use U.S. Food and Drug Administration terms such as "Red 219.") According to the public relations director, the cosmetics company had decided to offer the money to cover the women's medical and transportation costs but did not admit to any company guilt. He said that the company wanted to settle the matter and demonstrate its concern, even though it was not clear what had caused the women's problems. By the time that the settlements were reached in the Osaka case, most of the women's skin conditions had cleared up. The companies found it cheaper to settle with the plaintiffs than to permit the bad publicity to continue damaging their reputations.

Hospitals now have tests to show what is causing a woman's skin problems; manufacturers cannot refute charges when the tests clearly indicate that the fault lies in some ingredient they are using in their products, but a company often claims that a woman who complains is trying to blackmail it into paying hush money. Many women, said the consumer group, believe it may be some cosmetic they are using that causes their skin problem but have no way of proving it; many blame themselves for using cosmetics instead of blaming the cosmetic companies. It has been established that *kokuhisho*, black skin syndrome, is related to the use of the coal-tar dye Red 219, and that was the major problem in the Japanese cosmetic scandal of the mid-1970s. Red 219 was used by many companies, including companies selling door to door. There are seventy such Japanese door to door cosmetic companies employing some two hundred thousand salespeople.

One of the women who attended the July 1975 meeting at Osaka was Toshie Ohka of Kyoto, a city noted for its beautiful women. Mrs. Ohka had grown up looking like a *geisha* and was accustomed to seeing women wearing makeup. She had started using ABC cosmetics before the war, buying them from a man who said the products were so expensive because they were the best in the world. She continued buying them after the war, even when there was barely enough money for food, because the salesman was so persuasive. In 1963, the salesman recommended an ABC night cream, and Mrs. Ohka began using it, but after two or three times her skin began to get itchy. Wrinkles appeared about her eyes, and her entire face became dark red. She went to see a doctor and he told her she had *kokuhisho* — black skin syndrome. He gave her a shot and some medication, but after a year she could see no improvement. She complained to the ABC salesman, who came to her house with a cake and an apology. She lived with the condition for more than a dozen years, going to one doctor after another. At the 1975 meeting in Osaka, she learned that every time a woman complained about a cosmetic product she was told by the manufacturer that she was somehow unique, that the fault was in some physical peculiarity on her part, not in the product. Going to dermatologists, she encountered more and more women with skin problems and decided to write about her experience. A woman's face, she said, is very important, and she did not want other women to go through what she had endured.

Shioko Shirokawa, whose skin had always been nearly as free of blemishes as that of her daughter in high school, started to work part time and used EFG cosmetics, available only from beauty shops. Her beautician told her that dermatologists recommended the products because they did not contain certain perfumes to which many women were allergic. The beautician applied some EFG skin cream and explained that it was not expensive, that it contained ingredients to protect against sunburn, that it resisted perspiration, that it was more stable than some other skin creams, and that it was not necessary to apply very much. Mrs. Shirokawa bought a set of EFG products, liked them, and continued using them for two years. Then her skin began to dry up and flake like dandruff. She thought perhaps it was simply the change of season that was causing the dryness. Then she realized that her cheeks were getting darker, and she stopped putting rouge on her face. Soon she noticed that her upper lip was getting dark as if she had a moustache, and her chin was darkening as if she had a beard. Her family started to tease her, saying that she looked like a mountain bandit. Friends asked her what had happened to her face, and she never went out without makeup. Even with the makeup, her skin was so dark that she was embarrassed. At the beauty shop, she was told that she had a hormonal imbalance related to her age and recommended another cosmetic that was supposed to correct her problem. Desperate, Mrs. Shirokawa went to the hospital for a check-up. There was no physical problem, she discovered, and finally, in April 1972, she went to a dermatologist. He told her that he had seen women whose faces got darker because of the oil used in their cosmetics, but he did not know much about the problem or how to treat it. Eventually, Mrs. Shirokawa's face became infected and she started going to the hospital for treatments. After two months, she was referred to a dermatologist who told her she had black skin syndrome — *kokuhisho*. This was a common skin disorder among women in Europe and America after World War I, he said, because the women used certain skin creams, but he knew of no effective treatment.

After spending a good deal of time and money, Mrs. Shirokawa found a dermatologist who gave her a patch test and discovered that she was allergic to some ingredient in the cosmetics she was using. Ultra-violet ray treatments only made matters worse, and after another year she found a female physician who did an allergy test for each cosmetic product she used, including soaps and shampoos. The doctor explained that certain chemicals used in cosmetics were allergens. If used continually, they could discolor the skin, not just changing the surface, as ultraviolet rays do, but actually changing the pigmentation. Sunburn peels off; pigmentation discolored by chemical allergens can remain discolored for years. Another physician, this one in a Tokyo hospital, told Mrs. Shirokawa that cosmetic manufacturers never explain what ingredients are used in their products, so that even if she knew what ingredients were producing her allergic reactions it would not help her. She had no choice but to stop using skin creams altogether. Mrs. Shirokawa wrote a letter to the editor of the *Asahi Shimbun*, Japan's (and the world's) largest daily newspaper. Many other women wrote in to say that they had had similar experiences.

Teruyo Haraguchi, an Osaka woman who had been using rouge made by another company, found in October 1974 that the product had been discontinued and started to use a PQR rouge.

After using the PQR product for three months, her skin became itchy where she had used the rouge. She scratched her cheeks in her sleep, and when she awoke her face was red from the scratching. Eventually, her cheeks looked as if they had been burned, and she went to a hospital, where she was told that she was allergic to cosmetics. When she called the Osaka area branch of PQR to complain, a representative went to her house with a cake as a gesture of apology. The office had an arrangement with a dermatologist at Sumitomo Hospital and had her see the doctor. He advised her that the rouge had caused her problem, and PQR sent a car to take her to the hospital for each visit. By March 1975, her face no longer itched but her cheeks had turned a dark, brownish red. The color continued to darken, and in November 1975 she went to the Osaka Medical School Hospital, where she was told she had *kokuhisho*. Teruyo Haraguchi became chairperson of *Keshohinkogai higaisha no kai* — the Organization of Cosmetic Victims.

Perhaps the most frightening case cited by the Association of Japanese Consumers was that of an unnamed thirty-six-year-old woman who used an XYZ cleansing cream twice a day, cleaning her face with tissue paper after massaging it and then using an astringent. The woman had been allergic to some other products, but had no problems after using this one and she liked the smooth appearance it gave her face. After two weeks, however, she developed a fever and a faster heartbeat. She also began having headaches and occasionally felt dizzy. Then she noticed that her face felt sticky after washing off the cleansing cream and astringent, and she thought that was rather strange, but her skin did look smooth and shiny, so she continued her makeup procedure. Within a few months, the skin all over her body was as smooth as if she had been a wax figure, she had no energy, and she was losing weight. Finally she went to a physcian. He told her she was having trouble with her pancreas, her gall bladder, and so forth. A month or so later, she woke up one morning to discover that her face had been bleeding during the night. Then a shiny piece of matter emerged from a hair follicle on her leg. She felt as if there were something under the skin of her face, too, and when she took a bath her face and neck got very red. A liquid exuded from her pores, and she was able to save some of it. The liquid dried up after a few days, leaving a granule that looked very much like the matter that had emerged from the pore on her leg. The woman became so agitated that her family became concerned that she was having a nervous breakdown. More than ten physicians examined her at the hospital before a researcher in pharmaceuticals at the Tokyo City Office found a parrafin-like polymer — a chemical substance used to make enamel paints, artificial leather, and the like — in the XYZ cleansing cream. The astringent that the woman used had dissolved the polymer and permitted it to penetrate her skin and enter her bloodstream. It was preventing her pores from breathing. Even worse, it was affecting her internal organs.

Not until August 1979 did the Japanese Ministry of Health and Welfare act to require that cosmetic product ingredients be listed on the package (jar, tube, or bottle). According to an article published August 27, 1980, in the newspaper *Nippon Keizei Shimbun*, not all ingredients — only those that might cause problems — had to be listed. For most products that meant only two or three ingredients, although it could be as many as twenty. To an existing list of four hundred and thirty-four ingredients that might produce allergic reactions or worse, the government added another five hundred and gave companies until the fall of 1982 to meet the new regulation. Products had to be recalled from the shops and relabeled at considerable expense to the cosmetic companies. If the old package was too small to be relabeled, the product would have to be repackaged. Consumer organizations protested that the government had been too soft on the cosmetic companies in not requiring that all ingredients be listed. According to an article in the *Asahi Shimbun* of September 15, 1980, the companies protested that if all ingredients were listed it would put off consumers upset by chemical names and would affect sales. A very large company, with hundreds of products in its line, was hardest hit. It was estimated by the *Nippon Keizei Shimbun* that relabeling would cost that company ten percent of its annual sales revenues.

41. The typical female office clerk in Japan (the English term "Office Lady" and the abbreviation "O.L." are commonly used) is a high school or junior college graduate who lives at home or (rarely) in a company dormitory and who works only three to six years before marrying a middle-class male office worker or junior executive ("salaried man," or *sarariman*, is the term generally used), or

making a marriage arranged by her parents through a *nakaudo* (*see* note 18), and beginning her "important" role of raising children and managing the household. Her office job has little status or responsibility (even a four-year college graduate may be asked when applying for an Office Lady job if she is willing to serve tea as part of her duties), and her pay is extremely low as compared with that of her male counterpart. When a labor union official heard that some women had complained about having to serve tea, he said he saw nothing wrong with the rule. His wife served tea; why should Office Ladies not serve tea? Higher positions open to the men are not available to these Office Ladies; in fact, they are expected to perform "womanly" duties, such as serving tea, to make working conditions more pleasant for the men. Office Ladies are in some cases married women who have remained at work after the birth of their children. And a few Office Ladies are older single, widowed, or divorced women, although it is hard to see how anyone could support herself on the meager earnings of such a job.

The Office Lady is a relatively new phenomenon in Japanese history. When women first entered the Japanese work force in the late Nineteenth century, they began as unskilled workers, first in the textile industry, then in heavy industry as it developed. A girl working in a cotton or silk mill earned the equivalent of less than fifteen cents per day, and the company took eight cents out for her food. The companies paid the girl's parents a given amount when she was hired, sometimes when she was only seven or eight, and a percentage of this amount was also deducted from her wages, leaving her with almost nothing. In 1886, the Association of Silk Mills set a fifteen-hour day, from four-thirty in the morning until seven-thirty in the evening and cut wages by ten sen per day. This produced the first strike by women in Japanese history. Hundreds of girls from the Amamiya Silk Mill at Kofu in Yamanashi Prefecture assembled at a nearby temple and refused to work until their wages were restored and their hours reduced to the normal twelve hour shifts. Japanese industry employed one hundred and twenty thousand women in 1886. By 1894, Japan had three hundred and eight thousand factory workers, of whom two hundred and forty thousand were women.

At the turn of the century, wages were small for men as well as women; to help support their families, women worked at what were called *naishoku* — rolling cigarettes, labeling matchboxes, covering lampshades, making envelopes, hemming handkerchiefs, making paper fans, and so forth on a piecework basis at home in what Westerners call "cottage industries." Rice at that time sold for thirteen sen per *sho* (3.8 pints), and a woman had to label twelve hundred matchboxes, which generally took two days, to make twelve sen. Many women even in modern Japan work at *naishoku*. An *Asahi Shimbun* story in January 1978 noted that women worked at home making bicycle and toy parts, addressing envelopes, knitting, and so forth at piecework rates. The women earned about one hundred yen (fifty cents) per hour, or about ten thousand yen (fifty dollars) per month.

In 1904, Japan had five hundred and thirty thousand factory workers, of whom three hundred and ten thousand were women, eighty percent of them tending spindles in the textile mills and earning wages based on whether their ability put them in the first grade or the second grade. One *sho* of rice (3.8 pints) cost twenty sen, yet a girl made only twenty-five sen per day in the top grade, 14.3 sen in the lower grade. The Japanese economy depended on textile exports, and the textile factories depended on cheap labor. Their workers were mostly daughters of poor farmers. Japanese farmland is measured in terms of *tan*, one *tan* being just under a quarter-acre, and more than forty percent of farmers had less than a *gotan* (five *tans*, or 1.23 acres). Cheap as their labor was, mill owners kept trying to make it cheaper. On June 8, 1912, the *Manchoho Shimbun* published a letter from a girl working for a large textile company. Addressed to the president of the company, her letter said, "Please help me. I work at Tokyo Boseki. Until last year, we started work at six in the morning and worked until six in the evening, twelve hours. Starting in March, we have had to work eighteen hours a day. We have had to start at eleven in the evening and work until six the next morning, with only one hour off to eat and rest. My body is so tired that I cannot sleep."

In September 1916, a special law forbade hiring of children under age twelve except in special cases wehre the employer provided education. Working hours were limited to twelve, with one hour off. The law provided for two days off per month, which meant that people worked two Sundays out of the four in a typical month. Children from twelve to fifteen were considered *hogoshokko*, or protected workers, and were given special protection: they could not work night shifts except in alternate weeks, they got four days off per month, and they had to be paid every month, with the employer responsible for making sure that the child saved some money. Where many young girls were employed, the employer had to have a woman supervisor. In employee dormitories, boys and girls had to be kept separate and the employer had to provide each worker with space equal to half a *tatami* mat with his or her own *futon*. Sheets had to be provided as well as *futons*, the bedding had to be aired twice a month in the sun, and sleeping quarters had to be kept warm, although kerosene lamps were forbidden. Toilets had to be provided, and also a health clinic. Emergency exits were required for factories and dormitories, and it was forbidden to lock doors from the outside. If an employee became ill or hurt himself, the employer had to provide money for him to return home. The law applied only to factories with more than fourteen workers, but factory owners fought the law with such vigor that it did not become effective for twenty years. The record in Europe and the United States is not much better.

By 1920, when Tokyo buses started using women conductors, Japan had four million gainfully employed women, but only 12.5 percent were employed in offices. Women made about one-third as much as men doing the same work in those days. In 1930, when the Great Depression engulfed Japan along with other countries, the huge textile company Kanebo Boseki wanted to lay off women workers, most of whom could not go home if they lost their jobs. Twenty-six hundred girls remained in their dormitory, refusing to work or to leave. By 1974, 31.7 percent of Japanese working women were employed in offices as compared with 26.7 percent on factory assembly lines. Beginning in 1955, the number of women in the Japanese work force has been increasing steadily, and at a much faster rate than the number of men in the work force. In 1960, there were 7,160,000 female workers in Japan; that figure nearly doubled in the next twenty years to 13,540,000. The increase has been especially notable in service industries and sales jobs (both retail and wholesale).

In 1960, 36.1 percent of Japan's female workers were employed in manufacturing; by 1975, only 29.6 percent were employed in manufacturing, and by 1980 it was down to 27.1 percent and the service industry for the first time surpassed manufacturing, accounting for 29.6 percent of women's jobs as compared with 26.1 percent in 1960. The wholesale and retail trade employed 19.9 percent of the female work force in 1960, 25.9 percent in 1980. As for the specific jobs held by women, in 1960 more than thirty-six percent of female employees were craftworkers, production line workers, or laborers, while only 22.6 percent did clerical and related work, 9.1 percent were professional or technical workers, and nine percent were sales workers. By 1980, women doing clerical and related work ranked first, accounting for 33.1 percent, with craftworkers, production line workers, and laborers at 26.5 percent, professional and technical workers at 13.9 percent, and sales workers at 11.4 percent.

Women comprised 33.8 percent of the Japanese work force in 1980, but only 19.8 percent of working women had permanent jobs. The rest were considered "supplementary" and could be laid off at any time, thus making it possible for management to give their male counterparts lifetime employment. Despite the law that requires equal pay for equal work, the index for women's average wages in a 1980 government survey was 54.9 points as compared with one hundred for men. Ten years earlier, the index for women's wages was ten points lower. The gap has narrowed, but it is still enormous.

To be fair, it must be noted that most Japanese women still quit after working for three years. In 1978, Marubeni Corporation hired seventy-nine female four-year college graduates but treated them no differently from high school and junior college graduates, assigning them mostly to branch offices rather than to jobs in the main office. Although the company started a special examination program so that women could move into jobs equal to those held by men, it received no requests from young women to take the examinations. The *Yomiuri Shimbun* reported in March 1979 that major Japanese companies prefer women graduates from Jochi University, Aoyamagakuin, and Rikkyo University, all of whose graduates obtain employment. Sixty percent of Aoyamagakuin women get jobs at big banks, trading companies, and insurance companies, said the newspaper, and although the companies ask the women to work for at least three years, the average is under three. A woman who has completed four years of college is close to the upper limit of what is considered marriageable age and most women stop working when they are married. Women graduates complain that many companies are more concerned with a woman's appearance than with her ability and that companies often insist that a woman live with her parents rather than in her own apartment. The companies in many cases reply that they feel a responsibility toward *yomeirimae* (unmarried women) and do not want anything to happen to them, but many women come from the country and cannot live with their parents if they are to work for a large company in the city. A survey of one thousand 1973-1975 graduates of Kyoritsu University, a woman's institution with both two-year and four-year curricula, indicated that twenty-six percent of junior college graduates retired from work before three years, whereas sixty-one percent of four-year college graduates retired before three years. One reason that many companies do not want to hire women who are four-year college graduates is that they are older and will quit earlier to marry.

Professional jobs held by Japanese women are mostly in public health, private nursing, and teaching. For a woman who is not young, the only job opening may be as a cleaning woman or janitor.

Jack Seward, a U.S. military intelligence officer in World War II who married a Japanese woman after the war and lived in Japan for many years, has written several books attempting to explain the Japanese. In the last of these (*America and Japan: The Twain Meet.* Tokyo: Lotus Press, 1981), Seward, no feminist, quoted a woman professor, Chie Nakane, on the subject of discrimination against women: "Postwar and present-day discrimination against Japanese women is due to the nature of the labor market and the lack of experience of women in newly accessible job areas. Yet these disadvantages are often simplistically viewed as sheer sex discrimination... It is my view that among the Japanese sex consciousness has never been as strong as among the Americans."

Looking at the facts, many readers will agree with that judgment. In a three-year study submitted to the U.S. Equal Opportunity Commission in September 1981, the National Research Council said that American women were paid less than sixty cents for every dollar paid to men, although traditional work force patterns, not necessarily sex discrimination, accounted for the wide disparities. According to figures reported by the U.S. Department of Labor in March 1982, women hold 90.6 percent of bookkeeping jobs in the

United States and average ninety-eight dollars per week less than men holding the same jobs. Male administrators of elementary and secondary schools average five hundred and twenty dollars per week as compared with three hundred and sixty-three dollars for women holding the same jobs. Women hold 82.2 percent of elementary school teacher jobs yet average sixty-eight dollars less per week than male elementary school teachers. Male computer systems analysts average five hundred and forty-six dollars per week, female analysts four hundred and twenty dollars. Women hold 68.5 percent of the health technician jobs in American hospitals and clinics, yet they average only two hundred and seventy-three dollars per week as compared with three hundred and twenty-four dollars for male health technicians in comparable jobs. The executive director of Working Woman, an organization of two thousand women office workers, said the Labor Department figures supplied new evidence of discrimination in the workplace. A Labor Department employment analyst said the ratios were roughly consistent with what had been reported over a long period of time.

Less than one percent of full-time American working women earn twenty-five thousand dollars a year or more, according to Thelma Kandel's 1981 book *What Women Earn*, whereas twelve per cent of men earn that much. Two-thirds of U.S. women working full time earn less than ten thousand dollars per year. The median annual salary for an American male college graduate is $19,433 as compared to $12,028 for a female college graduate. Only one out of ten female workers earns as much as males in similar jobs. The average full-time employed woman earns just fifty-nine cents for every dollar earned by men. Women in technical and professional jobs earn less than seventy-one percent of men's median weekly salaries. Although a woman chemist may be paid a starting salary comparable to that of a man, in forty years she will be earning nearly nineteen thousand dollars less than the same man. In other words, discrimination against women occurs everywhere, not just in Japan.

42. The adoption of the Christian sabbath day by a people of Buddhist and Shinto faith antedates General MacArthur's regime in postwar Japan. It began in Japan's rush to Westernize during the Meiji era, a time during which the Gregorian calendar of 1582 was adopted; when Japanese men started wearing European morning

coats for formal occasions (male guests at important Japanese weddings and other major social functions still dress like English diplomats in the days of Gladstone and Queen Victoria); and when many Western words and customs were Japonized. In addition to Western calendar years, the Japanese continue to designate years according to the year of the emperor's reign. The emperor Hirohito succeeded to the imperial throne in 1926 and began the third reign since the Meiji restoration in 1868. His reign is called the Showa Period (his father's was the Taisho Period), and 1982 is Year Fifty-Seven of the Showa era.

43. Even today, most business in Japan is conducted in cash transactions rather than with checks or credit cards, although credit card use is increasing. One reason the Japanese stick to cash is that they are not accustomed to signing their names. A businessman customarily marks documents with a stamp (*han*) of wood, ivory, amethyst, or water buffalo horn bearing the characters of his name, and a *han* is easily counterfeited. Carrying large amounts of cash is relatively safe in Japan, given that country's low crime rate (*see* note 13), but when the Japanese go abroad they often forget that the rest of the world is not so safe. In the fall of 1981, Los Angeles County authorities wrote a letter to the Japanese consul general at Los Angeles suggesting that Japanese tourists traveling in the United States be warned not to carry cash. Kazuyoshi Miura, the proprietor of a Tokyo accessory shop, had been shot by a holdup man in central Los Angeles November 18 and was reported in critical condition. His wife Kazumi had also been shot, and the letter from the local authorities noted that criminals in the area were aware that Japanese tourists customarily carry large amounts of cash.

Back in Japan, news of the letter brought comments from people in the tourist industry that the Americans were obviously afraid of a decline in the number of Japanese tourists visiting the United States. It was reported that as many as three hundred thousand Japanese visited the U.S. West Coast each year, and a huge influx was expected for the 1984 Olympics at Los Angeles, where tourism is a six billion dollar industry even in normal years. In another widely publicized incident in the fall of 1981, a Tokyo man, who had been robbed on a previous visit to Los Angeles, returned to testify against the robbery suspect and was robbed again when he got to the city. As of late February 1982, Kazumi Miura was back in Japan and was still in a coma, unaware that she had been widowed. The Los Angeles Police Department had taken a young cop off the beat and put him in charge of a program, scheduled to take full effect by late March or early April, that was designed to reduce the vulnerability of tourists to the city's criminal element. The young officer was Jim Slater, who had brought the matter to the attention of his superiors. As patrolman Slater told à *New York Times* reporter, "It's very sad to take a report from a family who's come here for a vacation and to see how they have been ripped off of practically everything they had. Some of the tourists might as well wear a sign that says, 'Please rob me.'" Unaware of the dangers, tourists from Japan went on Beverly Hills shopping sprees carrying five thousand dollars or more in cash and travelers checks. They toured high-crime areas at night with expensive cameras slung round their necks. Muggers found them prime targets in Hollywood and in the downtown hotels favored by Japanese tour companies. After studying the problem, Slater concluded that for every reported crime committed against Japanese visitors, three were not reported. The program to help the tourists was supposed to include a film to be shown on flights from Japan to Los Angeles with tips on how to avoid being robbed. The script was written, but before filming began the Japanese tour companies scrapped the idea, saying it might scare away tourists. Habits are not easily changed; many Japanese tourists still carry a lot of cash when they visit the United States; many still become crime victims.

44. The hot bath, or *furo*, is a Japanese institution and passion, a source of tranquil relaxation as much as a cleansing experience. In the summer, a long soak in a tub of water heated to between one hundred and five and one hundred and ten degrees Fahrenheit makes the heat of the day (or evening) seem less oppressive. In the winter, an unheated house seems less chilly after a half hour in the *furo*. Soaking in the *furo* is preceded by thorough scrubbing with soapy rags and rinsing with fresh water splashed from pails or buckets as one stands on the well-drained tile floor outside the tub. The bather is clean before he or she enters the *furo*, and the hot water in the *furo* is retained for the next member of the family who uses it. (As a matter of courtesy, a guest is invited to go first.) This reuse of the hot water conserves energy; and since it would take a long time

to refill the tub for each bather, it is a practical necessity. A shower is more sanitary than a Western bath, in which one sits in one's own dirty water, but a Japanese *furo* is quite hygienic by virtue of the fact that its users are clean before they get into it. There is also the fact that the tub is usually filled to overflowing, so a certain amount of the previous user's water spills over, carrying with it some impurities, as the next user enters the tub.

Millions of urban Japanese still live in houses that have no baths. They depend on *sento* (public baths), as Japanese have for centuries, and these communal facilities are to be found in every town and in all parts of every city. Despite the popular Western misconception, the sexes are generally separated in the public baths, although there is still mixed bathing at a few hot springs resorts. For *samurai* families, the baths were always segregated. For the common people, separation began only in the years after Commodore Perry's expedition opened Japan to Western ideas (*see* note 69). An Ensign McCauly, whose values were typically Victorian, was among Perry's sailors and recorded in his diary, "I went into a bath house where girls of seventeen, old women, young women, old men were squatting on the stone floor, without rag enough to cover a thumbnail…they invited us to join and take a wash — but I was so disgusted with the whole breed, with their lewdness of manner and gesture, that I turned away with a hearty curse upon them." In 1862, Yokohama officials responded to criticism by resident foreigners, including no doubt some Christian missionaries; it banned mixing the sexes in public baths. Elsewhere in Japan, most public baths continued to be mixed for nearly ninety years and it was not until 1964, the year of the Tokyo Olympics, that the police enforced segregation in the *onsen* (hot springs) establishments. (Japan has thirteen thousand three hundred hot springs of which fourteen hundred have mineral properties said to be of medicinal value.)

While paying the fee to enter a *sento* (public bath) in Japan today, one can in most cases still catch a fleeting glimpse of both sides of the partition that separates the sexes (the cashier sits at a counter overlooking both sides). The *sento* open at three o'clock in the afternoon (that is when mothers often bring their babies to take advantage of the cleanest water) and close at eleven thirty at night. The fees are modest — about two hundred and twenty yen (roughly one dollar) for an adult, ninety yen for a child of six to fifteen, forty yen for a younger child —and while the popularity of public baths has declined with the growth of apartment complexes in which each apartment has its own bath, some people still find the spaciousness of the *sento* more relaxing.

45. That so many people have written so many books attempting to explain the success of Japanese industry without ever mentioning the name Deming is hard to understand. W. Edwards Deming of Washington, D.C., still setting a fast pace at age eighty-one as this was written, is known as a quality control expert. He is actually a mathematical statistician, and he more than anyone else is responsible for the fact that "Made in Japan" is today a mark of quality whereas the term once meant quite the opposite. Dr. Deming is revered in Japan, where Emperor Hirohito has awarded him the Second Order Medal of the Sacred Treasure for his contributions to the economy. Only in recent years have some Americans begun to realize what Deming's ideas are and how much they have helped Japanese industry become the great power that it is.

When industrial production resumed in Japan after World War II, a seller's market encouraged companies to produce goods in quantity with little regard to quality. General MacArthur was the *de facto* ruler of the nation, and most Japanese industrialists aspired only to regain their prewar position, which in world markets was not very strong. Only when General MacArthur's office retained Deming as an adviser in sampling techniques in 1947 did some Japanese industrialists realize the importance of statistical ideas and methods.

Deming was a disciple of the late Dr. Walter A. Shewhart, a statistician who had published a book in 1931 showing that random variability represents the ultimate state of any system, including a manufacturing system. A manufacturer wants every product coming off his line to be of uniform quality. This is impossible. It is inevitable that some products will be slightly better or worse than others. Most manufacturers do not know how to measure the deviation from uniform quality. Until a manufacturer achieves the state of random variability and has an identifiable process, he has chaos, often to a high degree. Nonrandom variability has assignable causes. These can usually be charged to particular, local conditions that workers can recognize and eliminate. What is left after they are eliminated is random variability, which has common causes such as poor lighting, humidity, vibration, poor food in the cafeteria, absence of a real quality program, poor supervision, raw material of poor or spotty quality, and so forth. Workers have no control over these common causes, and they are more difficult to identify than are special causes. Shewhart had shown that only management can improve random variability. Deming then developed principles that went beyond Shewhart's contribution. Inspection does not assure quality, he said, quality must be built in. Searching out the cause of every product defect will only perpetuate the problem of product defects. New machinery or new equipment will not eliminate manufacturing headaches; it simply produces a new set of headaches. Without using statistical methods, a manufacturer cannot understand what is wrong with his system and will not be able to improve his productivity. The manufacturer may blame certain workers or certain machines although such factors rarely account for more than fifteen percent of his trouble. What is mostly to blame is the system, said Deming, and the responsibility for that must be borne by management, not labor.

"A prophet is not without honor, save in his own country, and in his own house," says the Book of Matthew (13:57). Such was the reception of Shewhart's and Deming's ideas in the United States. However, some Japanese recognized that there was a lot to what Deming said. Sensitive to the poor image of Japanese products in world markets, the Union of Japanese Scientists & Engineers (JUSE), or Nippon Kagaku Gijutsu Renmei, sponsored a quality control seminar in September 1949. The JUSE learned toward the end of the year that Deming would return to Japan in May 1950 as adviser in sampling techniques to General Headquarters, SCAP. It was known that Stanford University had, at Deming's suggestion, given American engineers eight-day courses in statistical techniques to help the war effort, and JUSE's managing director, Ken-ichi Koyanagi, wrote to Deming early in 1950 asking the pioneer of statistical quality control to give a brief lecture course to Japanese research workers, plant managers, and engineers.

Deming agreed to give a series of lectures and refused any remuneration. When the first eight-day course on "Elementary Principles of the Statistical Control of Quality" was given in mid-

July 1950, two hundred and thirty men were exposed to Deming's ideas. In the next twenty years, JUSE trained nearly fifteen thousand engineers and thousands of plant foremen in elementary statistical methods. And as Japanese exports of material goods increased, so did Japanese exports of statistical knowledge and methods. In the 1950s, nearly one-third of the abstracts selected for the *International Journal of Abstracts on Statistical Methods in Industry* came from Japan.

The men who heard Deming in 1950 were electrified by his prediction that Japanese products would invade world markets within five years and that Japan's standard of living would soon be equal to that in the world's most prosperous countries. At that time, much of Japan's work force was engaged in agriculture. Deming observed that if Japanese goods could find markets abroad, it would not be necessary for the nation to be self-sufficient in the production of food. In fact, it might be more intelligent for Japan to concentrate more labor in manufacturing and to export manufactured goods while importing food. At least two years would be needed to revise Japanese ideas of quality, precision, and uniformity, Deming told his listeners, and at least another five years to establish a reputation for quality, precision, and uniformity. Patience and long-range planning would be necessary if the Japanese were to overcome the prewar reputation that "Made in Japan" meant inferior quality. Japanese manufacturers would have to use consumer research in their export markets to guide the design, manufacture, and marketing of their products, and they would have to act in concert. Using statistical methods only here and there would not pull the country out of its crisis. Top management throughout Japan would have to work together in an effort that would leave no doubt as to the improved quality and dependability of Japanese merchandise. Finally, Japan might be poor in natural resources — little oil, little coal, iron ore, some wood —but she was rich in the greatest resource of all. She had a skilled and willing labor force. She had engineers, statisticians, and economists whose technical knowledge was unsurpassed. Statistical methods and other technical advances could save so much scarce material that the savings would be tantamount to finding new deposits of coal, iron ore, copper, oil, and other basic raw materials. Deming had seen one company use statistical methods to cut its fuel use by nearly one third; he had seen another improve one operation to decrease loss in scrap to one ninth of what it had been.

Some Japanese companies had guaranteed lifetime employment to workers before World War II. Many more companies did so in the fierce competition for labor after the war. But Japanese labor harmony is due as much to Deming's evidence that systems (meaning management), and not labor, are responsible for most production faults as is guaranteed lifetime employment. If purchasing agents make price their chief criteria in buying raw materials, labor can hardly be blamed for an increase in the percentage of rejects. If top management bends all its efforts to increasing the next quarterly dividend rather than to ensuring the long-term viability of the company, lower productivity is not the fault of labor. By taking the onus off labor, Deming's principles made it easier for labor and management to work together. Recent studies by consultants, academicians, and American automobile companies indicate that major Japanese automobile makers can manufacture and ship a small car to the United States for thirteen hundred to seventeen hundred dollars less than it costs General Motors, Ford, or Chrysler to produce a similar car. True, the hourly wage and benefit rates that a G.M. worker receives come to $19.65 versus eleven dollars at Toyota, but according to a study made by one American management consultant, the hourly labor cost difference is probably less than five hundred dollars per car (some studies have said five hundred and fifty dollars), and that is nearly offset by the shipping and duty costs of bringing a car from Japan to the United States, so Detroit's dilemma cannot be blamed on high hourly wage rates. According to the study cited, more efficient manufacturing methods still give the Japanese an advantage of about fifteen hundred dollars per car. The *kanban* method employed by Toyota and other Japanese automakers involves keeping inventories of parts to an absolute minimum, whereas General Motors carries about nine billion dollars in worldwide inventories at an estimated cost of three billion dollars, including storage, handling, staffing, freight charges, and losses due to obsolescence or defects. Japanese automakers, moreover, rely on fewer suppliers (Toyota uses fewer than two hundred and fifty while General Motors uses more than thirty five hundred), and they make sure that each step of the manufacturing process is done correctly the first time even if it means that the assembly line runs more slowly, and continually reduce the amount of human labor that goes into each car. These methods are based in large part on what the Japanese learned from E. W. Deming.

Deming donated all royalties from the Japanese edition of his *Elementary Principles of the Statistical Control of Quality* to Ken-ichi Koyanagi of the Union of Japanese Scientists & Engineers (JUSE). With these royalties as its basic fund, JUSE resolved in December 1950 to create the Deming Prize as a means of honoring Deming's contribution and for the encouragement of quality control development in Japan, and prizes have been awarded once a year almost every year since 1951. Beginning in 1953, the newspaper *Nihon Keizai Shimbun Sha* (better known as *Nikkei*) began donating funds for the Deming Prize in research and education, which goes to individuals who have excelled in theoretical research and application of quality control, something substantially more than just a silver medal. The Deming Prize for Application is awarded to corporations or plants that have attained notable results in the practice of quality control.

A company vying for a Deming Prize generally makes a deliberate effort to capture the prize, setting its goal years in advance and working methodically toward achieving that goal. This kind of long-range planning is characteristic of Japanese industry and reflects the stability of management as compared to American management, which often seems to work on the principle of the Hollywood star system with executives trying to score personal triumphs that will win them higher positions in other companies. This principle necessarily focuses efforts on short-term objectives at the expense of a company's future welfare.

Creating "constancy of purpose in the company" is, in fact, number one on Deming's list of fourteen points for top management today. The next quarterly dividend, he says, is not as important as the existence of the company ten, twenty, or thirty years from now. He urges management to innovate, to allocate resources for long-term planning, to invest in research and education, and to put resources into maintaining equipment and buying new aids for increased productivity in the office and in the plant. Point number two on Deming's list: learn the new philosophy and stop accepting defective materials and poor workmanshp as a way of life. Point number three: require statistical evidence of process control along with incoming critical parts. Japanese companies, says Deming, work with their suppliers to make sure that quality is built in rather than buying from the low bidder. Statistical control provides the only way that a supplier can build in quality, predict his costs, and provide a purchaser with evidence of consistent and uniform quality and of production costs. Some suppliers follow their product through the purchaser's production line to learn what problems turn up so that they can move to avoid such problems in the future. Some of them can talk in pertinent statistical language, a language that purchasing agents must learn. While Japanese manufacturers hold suppliers to tight delivery schedules and high quality standards, American manufacturers spend billions of dollars on storing and financing inventories of parts and materials supplied on loose delivery schedules and of uncertain quality.

Listening to Deming, one gets the impression that Japanese management exercises leadership while American management (including the giant defense procurement bureaucracy) generally runs scared, wastes its energy on internal politics, tries to protect itself from recriminations, and in many cases doesn't really know what it is trying to accomplish. Lower level managers pretend that they know their jobs because if they ask questions they may be thought incompetent. It has been shown that eighty percent of American workers do not know what their jobs are and they are afraid to ask.

Many people point to Japan's quality control circles in which workers discuss production methods with their foremen and they suggest that American industry should emulate these quality control circles. They generally fail to recognize that the Japanese method is effective only within a larger context in which management takes a longer view than typical Western management; in which purchasing managers look for more than low prices; in which workers are not afraid to ask questions; in which everyone is working for the common good rather than for personal glory; and in which government and business are not eternal adversaries.

47.   *Ms.* magazine began publication at New York in July 1972. *Ms.* promotional writer Phyllis Langer worked until three days before her daughter Alix was born August 23, 1973. Five weeks later, she was back at the office every Monday, Wednesday, and Friday with Alix, a portable bed, three boxes of disposable diapers, and a case of

baby formula. Alix was still coming to the office in March 1975, when *Ms.* ran a cover story on the little girl, and by that time a member of the art staff, Cindy Nagel, was bringing her son Joshua to work every day. The magazine's art director Barbara Richer gave birth March 31, 1976, to a son, Ian, and returned to work two and a half months later, bring Ian with her. This was at the request of the magazine. There had been no problems with Alix or Joshua and nobody saw any reason why Ian should be any trouble, either. Taking the baby to the office is still not the norm anywhere in the world, but in its March 1975 cover story on little Alix Langer, *Ms.* carried an article about Susan Catania, a member of the Illinois State Legislature, who brought her fifth daughter, Amy, to the House each day during the period that she was breast-feeding. Catania was head of the Illinois Commission on the Status of Women. The atmosphere in the general assembly was far from totally formal, she said. "There is always a lot of conversation, eating, and newspaper-reading during sessions, so having a small child or two on the floor is hardly disruptive. Recently, a few men started bringing their very young children. It's very encouraging." When asked if there had been any temper tantrums on the floor of the House, Catania replied, "Only from legislators." Most American companies say that their employee liability insurance bars infants and toddlers from the office.

48.   *Shufunotomo* (the name means *Housewife's Companion*) began publication in March 1917, when most Japanese women still wore kimono. This is the magazine whose interview with Nancy Reagan in January 1981 led to the forced resignation of U.S. national security adviser William V. Allen in November 1981. Allen, it was alleged, had set up the five-minute interview and had accepted one thousand dollars plus two wristwatches in return for his help. More than just a magazine, *Shufunotomo* publishes books and operates a women's apparel store. According to the magazine's chief editor Kyoko Fukao, *Shufunotomo* has more working mothers in editorial positions than most publishing houses. The magazine never encouraged married women to continue working, but had no policy against women employees getting married and having children. Company policy was never the problem; it was simply that most women found it too difficult to be an editor and also a mother. The

women employees try to help each other, and that, according to Fukao, is unique. According to another source, *Shufunotomo* winks at the law that forbids women to work late. When deadline pressures make it necessary, women work the same hours as men, even until midnight. But no *Shufunotomo* editor brings her baby to work.

49. Japanese schoolteachers obtained maternity leave as early as October 1922. Only thirty percent of pregnant working women take the maximum maternity leave permitted before the birth of a child. According to 1974 figures from the Department of Women and Juvenile Workers in the Ministry of Labor, five percent take less than seven days, twelve percent take eight to twenty-one days, 19.7 percent take twenty-two to fifty-five days, 36.5 percent take thirty-six to forty-two days. The 1947 Labor Standards Law forbids a company to let a mother return to work until six weeks after childbirth, or five weeks if she obtains approval from her physician. As is so often the case with Japanese statistics, figures on how soon mothers return to the job after childbirth do not add up: 58.1 percent of women given maternity leave return within six weeks of childbirth, 39 percent return later, according to the Ministry of Labor. Some Japanese companies today give *husbands* maternity leave of up to five days when their wives have children.

By some accounts, more than a third (34.2 percent) of Japanese companies provide full pay during maternity leave; other reports maintain that two-thirds pay nothing at all, although certain companies do provide some pay, depending on the agreement between the company and the union and on whether or not the company has a health insurance plan. Most companies do have such plans and pay half the amount of the premiums, the workers paying the other half. A woman on maternity leave generally receives 60 percent of her pay from the insurance plan, but a woman working for a small company without a plan receives nothing. In 1973, 48.8 percent of Japanese working women retired when they became pregnant or when their children were born. The figure is now almost certainly lower, partly because more families need the second income.

Under the terms of the 1947 Labor Standards Law, Japanese companies are supposed to provide time for working mothers to nurse their infants, allowing them to come in half an hour late in the morning and leave half an hour early in the evening or take half an hour off twice a day for breast-feeding. In practice, fewer than half of Japanese companies observe the law. The government-operated cigarette factories provide on-premise nurseries that look after infants and children while their mothers are working. This is hardly typical.

The Japanese Diet passed a law in 1975 providing for one year's leave without pay for schoolteachers, school clinic nurses, and nursery personnel to nurse their infants. Relatively few of the women affected could afford to give up all pay for that long and most returned to work after maternity leave or within a few months.

50. There is no federal law in the United States that protects pregnant or lactating women. State laws vary. Connecticut and Massachusetts provide for eight weeks' maternity leave — four weeks before childbirth, four weeks after. Vermont splits the eight weeks into two before childbirth, six after. New Jersey obliges companies to provide four weeks before childbirth and four after, with pay. Four weeks' leave after childbirth is the law in New York. Washington State provides for ten weeks, four before childbirth, six after. Oregon splits the ten weeks the other way but forbids a company to employ a pregnant or lactating woman without a doctor's permission. Rhode Island, which has a large Roman Catholic population, requires a company to give a woman fourteen weeks off with pay before childbirth if she is having a difficult pregnancy.

The country with the most generous law is Italy. In 1971, following labor union agitation, the Italian government established a law requiring two months' maternity leave before childbirth and three months after. If her work poses a danger to her pregnancy, the woman is entitled to three months' leave before childbirth. All maternity leave is paid at eighty percent of regular pay. During the first year of lactation, a working mother may take off one hour twice a day. If her child becomes ill during that first year, she may take six months' leave without losing her job. If the child becomes ill during the first three years, the mother may take a day off and not lose her job so long as she has a doctor's authority.

51. Social security benefits paid to Japanese women in 1979 averaged one-third the amounts paid to men, partly because women retire earlier than men and partly because contributions are based on pay and women had been paid at lower rates. The men averaged

¥ 107,800 per month (about five hundred dollars) and women only ¥ 35,600 (about one hundred and seventy dollars). During the Meiji Period, sixty to seventy percent of Japanese textile workers were females, and ten percent of them were under the age of fourteen. While child labor is no longer legal in Japan, the attitude toward working women has not changed much, in some respects, since the Meiji Period. Many young women went to work in Japanese factories during World War II because young men without handicaps were serving in the emperor's armed forces, but the women received only seventy-one percent of what the men had been making. Under the 1947 Labor Standards Law, an employer convicted of discriminating in pay on the basis of sex may be sentenced to a maximum of six months' imprisonment and a maximum fine of five thousand yen (about twenty-five dollars). In practice, relatively few companies observe the law of equal pay for equal work, yet it is unheard of for an employer to serve any time in prison for such an offense, and a fine of five thousand yen is hardly even a slap on the wrist.

In 1974, Japanese women averaged 53.9 percent as much pay as men. The comparable figure for France was 86.7 percent, for Australia 80.1 percent, for Denmark 77 percent, for West Germany 69.9 percent, for Switzerland 63.3 percent, and for Great Britain 60.7 percent. The Japanese average is lowered considerably by the fact that so many women quit after marriage or when they have their first child, but even in the case of single women the average pay is lower because Japanese companies consider women as temporary workers, or supernumeraries (*shokutaku*). Even a permanent female employee is called a temporary; she may do more work than her male counterpart, but she gets fewer benefits and lower pay. A clerk in the city government office at Suzuka City saw that her male junior was promoted at increased pay while her pay scarcely increased at all. Incensed, the woman spoke to other women in the office. In April 1971, about twenty women presented a letter to the city government, demanding equal treatment with regard to pay and promotion. The government replied that pay was based on the type of job and that there had been no discrimination based on sex. A year later, the woman saw that her junior had once again been promoted while she was still left in a lower grade. She took the case to court.

52.   Japan suffered about 1,500,000 military casualties in World War II plus hundreds of thousands of civilian casualties. The United States suffered more than 290,000 military casualties, almost no civilian casualties.

53.   *Ronin* were unemployed *samurai* during the Tokugawa and Meiji periods. The word has been appropriated to mean students not in regular schools but preparing for entrance examinations.

54.   An innovation introduced by the Americans, the P.T.A. succeeded a prewar Association of Parents (*fukei kai*), which included parents of all schoolchildren. Although the name really means "association of fathers and brothers," many mothers showed up at meetings. P.T.A. theoretically stands for Parent-Teachers Association, but in Japan it is largely a parents' organization with little teacher representation. Only parents who want to become members join American P.T.A.s; in Japan, every parent belongs automatically. Parents in Japanese P.T.A.s often belong to volleyball and dodgeball teams that play against parents of children in other classes.

55.   In 1978, Japan's Ministry of Education compared the sizes of twelve-year-old schoolchildren to sizes recorded in 1950. Girls in 1950 had averaged 137.3 centimeters (about fifty-four inches) in height, 32.6 kilograms (nearly seventy-two pounds) in weight. In 1978, twelve-year-old girls averaged 150.1 centimeters (just over fifty-nine inches) in height, 42.7 kilograms (more than ninety-four pounds) in weight. In 1950, boys had averaged 136.5 centimeters (just over fifty inches) in height (boys do not grow as quickly as girls at that age), 32.5 kilograms (71.65 pounds) in weight. In 1978, twelve-year-old boys averaged 149.6 centimeters (nearly fifty- nine inches) in height, forty-one kilograms (just over ninety pounds) in weight. Professor Yoshio Honda of Jikei Medical School has said that even Japanese noses are getting larger. Six-foot Japanese men are no longer uncommon, and the growth is generally ascribed to dietary factors. Children in Japan grow up eating far more protein than did children in pre-war generations, and the Japanese are simply attaining their "biological potential," to use the term employed by nutritionists. (Only genetics can explain why my wife

Chie, born in Japan before the war, is a hair taller than my full-grown daughter Amanda.)

56. Tokyo alone has more than six thousand *chirigami kokan*, most of whom work alone driving old trucks which they either own or rent by the day. The business is fiercely competitive, and owning a truck provides a slight profit advantage. In a country where a prospective employer is likely to ask a great many detailed personal questions, some men find few job openings except that of a *chirigami kokan*, which has neither social status nor job security, and many have been driven out of the business by slackening demand for wastepaper. Typically, a *chirigami kokan* will pick up fresh toilet paper from the junkyard to which he sells his wastepaper and will give a householder a free roll of paper for every twenty-two to twenty-six pounds of wastepaper. Compounding the problems of the *chirigami kokan* early in 1982 was a circulation drive by some *Yomiuri Shimbun* distributors. They sent people out in advance of the *chirigami kokan*, picked up subscribers' old newspapers, and gave them three to four times as much toilet paper, thus undercutting the junkyards as well as the toilet paper exchangers.

57. The Boys' Day Festival has been celebrated for centuries. Its origins lie in the bright banners and grotesque figures displayed by farmers during the Tokugawa period to frighten off crop-destroying insects in early May. The figures were later turned into representations of famous warriors, and instead of placed in the fields they were displayed indoors to inspire the boys in a family to emulate the bravery and fighting prowess of *samurai*. About 1772, tubular paper carp were flown from poles outdoors because it was felt that the indoor displays were not enough to glorify the *samurai* festival, and today, these paper carp may be seen in early May, appearing to swim upstream as they billow in the wind. The carp is said to exemplify courage, fortitude, and perseverance in overcoming obstacles, and the intent of the festival is to express the hope that every boy in the family will be healthy and vigorous enough to succeed in life. The carp is a long-lived fish and is often very colorful. Collectors pay high prices for prize specimens. Boys' Day coincides with the final day of kite fighting at Hamamatsu, in Shizuoka Prefecture, where the event has been held since about 1550 and is part of the Suwa Shrine Festival. This festival commemo-

rates the birth announcement by a feudal lord who wrote the name of his newborn son on a kite and flew it high in the sky so that all could see. Contestants fly huge kites with strings to which sharp objects or bits of glass have been added and try to cut the strings of their opponents' kites.

58.   Celebrating birthdays is a postwar innovation in Japan. Although the emperor's birthday was observed before World War II, ordinary Japanese became one year older on New Year's Day, a system employed in the West only for racehorses.

59.   Quarantine control officers at the airport said that the meat could not be imported without U.S. Department of Agriculture documents showing that it came from an animal free of foot-and-mouth disease. The United States employs the same procedure to prevent the spread of this disease. The Japanese gave me a receipt, kept the meat in a freezer until my departure, and then returned it to me. Fortunately, I had made a copy of the receipt and was able to persuade American officials that the meat had come from the United States; otherwise there would have been forty pounds of steak without a country.

60.   Konosuke Matsushita revolutionized Japanese cooking in 1946 with an electric rice saucepan — Japan's first low-priced electrical cooking appliance. He had begun his career in 1918 with a simple three-bulb light fixture and proceeded to develop a vast empire under the name National Panasonic when most Japanese entrepreneurs still insisted on naming their companies after themselves.

61.   The onetime diplomat Ichiro Kawasaki wrote in his 1969 book *Japan Unmasked* that the Japanese had a popular saying: "One is free from shame while on a trip." This, he said, explained why Japanese soldiers were able to commit such atrocities in China and Southeast Asia (later matched by American atrocities in Southeast Asia) and why the otherwise clean and tidy Japanese litter the floors of railway cars with empty lunch boxes, cigarette butts, ashes, empty bottles, and so much other trash that the sweepers cannot keep up with the

mess they make. "A Japanese has been subject from time immemorial to all sorts of regimentaions, both mental and otherwise, within his own family circle or his community," wrote Kawasaki. "For example, a young child is taught to behave unobtrusively in the presence of others and to be always polite to his elders. A young girl is also told to behave gently on all occasions for fear that 'others may laugh at you,' or if she is married, to do her utmost to please her fastidious 'in-laws.' In prewar days, a young girl even had to learn to sleep straight, with her legs together. Thus the Japanese are placed under constant mental restraint while at home in order to conform to prescribed etiquette and behavior. So once outside the confines of his home or family, a Japanese is at last 'liberated' from all these restraints and starts behaving like a different person... The degree of selfishness, rudeness, and inconsideration shown in public conveyances in Japan...cannot be surpassed. Such anti-social behavior of the Japanese can only be properly understood in the context I have just explained."

62.   There has been an explosion in the numbers of cars and trucks on Japan's inadequate roads. In 1960, the country had only 440,417 passenger cars, 1,321,601 trucks. By 1970, those numbers had risen to 6,776,949 and 5,460,393, respectively. Five years later, Japan had 14,882,193 cars and 7,381,024 trucks, and by 1980 there were 21,542,500 cars, 8,682,978 trucks. In 1960, when Tokyo had only sixty thousand automobiles as compared with several million today, the city's traffic congestion was probably even worse than it is now. Streets and avenues have been widened at enormous cost, freeways have been constructed, gardens have given way to garage space, and there are huge underground parking complexes.

63.   About sixty-two percent of the Japanese own their own homes.

64.   Only Sweden, Denmark, and the Netherlands have more bicycles per capita than Japan, which had about forty-seven million (one for every 2.3 people) in February 1979. When oil prices shot up that year and made driving to work by car more costly than ever, bicycle ownership increased further.

65. The *Hoshi* (Star) *Matsuri* (Festival), or *Tanabata* (Weaving Loom) *Matsuri*, is based on a Chinese T'ang dynasty legend involving two stars, *Kengyu* (the cowherd star) and *Shokujo* (the princess weaver star). The stars are on either side of the Milky Way, or *Ama-no-gawa*, the river of heaven, and modern astronomers call them Altair and Vega. According to the legend, the princess was a skillful and industrious weaver. Looking up from her work one day as she wove cloth for her father's royal robe, she saw a handsome cowherd tending his cows. It was love at first sight, and she set aside her weaving to meet the young man, who also fell in love. The king was not opposed to their marrying, but he was displeased when his daughter put aside her weaving and the cowherd let his cows go astray. This, in fact, so exasperated his majesty that he forced the young couple to remain on opposite sides of the Milky Way, permitting them to meet only one night of the year. With no bridge to cross the river of heaven, the princess weaver and the cowherd were melancholy until a magpie (*kasasagi*), who saw the princess crying, assured her highness that a bridge would somehow be found. On the evening when the couple were permitted to meet, the bird got other magpies to flock together and they formed a bridge with their outstretched wings, enabling the princess to cross over and meet with her cowherd lover.

It is recorded that *Tanabata Matsuri* was celebrated as early as the reign of the Empress Koken at Nara (749-758), and that the people of Edo (later Tokyo) began observing the festival sometime during the Tokugawa period that began in 1603. The emperors and their families had celebrated before then by composing poems, and it became the custom to hang strips of paper on bamboo branches and float them downstream on the festival day. If poems or proverbs were written on the strips of paper, it was believed that the writer would be more likely to improve his calligraphy; and if threads of bright colors were tied to the bamboo branches, the person who tied them would have a better chance of becoming a good weaver or seamstress. People prayed to the cowherd for good rice harvests and to the princess weaver for skill in handwriting, sewing, weaving, and other arts. According to the legend, the magpies were able to make their bridge of wings across the Milky Way only in fine weather; a rainy evening meant that the lovers would not be able to meet for another year, so people prayed, and still pray, for a clear evening.

Until the Meiji period, *Tanabata Matsuri* was observed on the seventh night of the seventh month of the lunar calendar. It is now celebrated on July 7, according to the Gregorian calendar. Schoolchildren write on paper strips and offer examples of their calligraphy to the two stars, and bamboo branches hung with poems written on colored strips of paper (*tanzaku*) are placed in front of houses or garden gates. On July 8, children take their decorated bamboo branches to the nearest stream for the current to carry away.

66.   By the end of third grade, a Japanese child must have mastered 881 of the two thousand basic Chinese *kanji* ideograms (*see* note 12) plus *hiragana* and *katakana*; by sixth grade he must know at least eighteen hundred.

67.   Japanese television broadcasting began February 1, 1953, when NHK (*Nippon Hoso Kyokai*, or Japanese Broadcasting Association) aired its first telecasts. NHK had begun as a pioneer radio company and had been reorganized on a non-profit basis in 1950. Stations of NHK's two TV networks outnumber stations affiliated with commercial television companies. According to Japanese figures, television set ownership in Japan is relatively low — 24.3 sets per hundred people as compared to 57.1 in the United States, 36.8 in Sweden, 36.6 in Canada, 33.8 in Denmark, 32.9 in the United Kingdom, 29.9 in West Germany, 28.5 in Switzerland, 27.9 in France, and 26.4 in New Zealand (1976-77 figures). NHK says that the average Japanese over age seven watches two hundred and seventeen minutes of TV on weekdays, two hundred and seventy-six minutes on Sundays.

68.   New York's Nichibei Fujinkai, one of several Japanese wives' associations in the city, arranges seating at its regular meetings in the order of the status held by the husbands of the women. The hierarchy in the community is rigid, and many wives become lonely and depressed. Relatively few consult psychiatrists because there is a stigma attached to psychiatry in Japan and the women are fearful

that their husbands' careers may suffer, or that their children may have trouble getting married, if it becomes known that someone in the family had a psychiatric problem. On the other hand, Japanese women in New York are sometimes astonished to discover that their skills are more marketable in a country where employment levels are determined more by merit than by seniority, and to find that American women tend to have less influence in their families than Japanese women, who are the traditional behind-the-scenes managers.

69.   Shimoda is the port town at which Japan's first American consul-general, Townsend Harris, made his home in the 1850s. Until Commodore Matthew Calbraith Perry of the U.S. Navy arrived at Edo (later Tokyo) in July 1853 with the first formal bid for United States relations with Japan, almost the only Westerners that any Japanese had seen in centuries were hostile Russians, rude Britons, shipwrecked sailors, or whalers putting in for repairs or food. The Dutch were permitted to maintain a small office on the island of Dejima off Nagasaki in Kyushu, and one or two Dutch vessels could come in each year with materials the Japanese needed. However, the Dutch merchants had to visit Edo periodically and make fools of themselves before the shogun. Their Japanese employees had to prove their hostility to Christianity once or twice a year by trampling on a cross (no religious services were permitted at Dejima).

This attitude toward foreigners had begun in 1587 when the Japanese dictator Hideyoshi Toyotomi invaded Kyushu to subjugate a defiant *daimyo*. Hideyoshi was refused a beautiful woman with whom to sleep because all the women had embraced Christianity. Furious, he issued an edict forbidding foreign missionaries, and in 1597 executed three Jesuits, six Franciscans, and seventeen Japanese Christians. The Tokugawa shogun Ieyasu who gained power two years after Hideyoshi's death in 1598 permitted some trade with the West but began a definite policy of persecuting Christians in 1612 and banned Christian missionaries from the country in 1614. William Adams, the English mariner who was forced to remain in Japan after his Dutch ship foundered in 1600, built ships that took him and his Japanese crews to Siam and Cochin China on trading expeditions between 1616 and 1618. That was the peak of Japan's foreign relations in the Tokugawa period. In 1636, the shogun Iemitsu, grandson of Ieyasu, forbade his people to travel abroad; at the end of the following year he began a siege to force the submission of his *daimyo* in Kyushu who had become a Christian.

Early in 1638 Iemitsu annihilated most of the thirty-seven thousand Christian peasants who had been holed up in Hara Castle near Nagasaki for three months. Iemitsu expelled Portuguese traders on suspicion of complicity in the uprising, which was actually supported by a Dutch vessel, and he sealed off Japan, prohibiting the construction of large ships that might carry people abroad.

Isolated from foreign "barbarians," Japan had no steam engines, no forge capable of casting a cannon, no modern firearms, no fortifications other than earthworks armed with ancient cannon, no ships larger than fifty-foot junks, no telegraph, and no new fashions in wearing apparel. Japanese men and women still dressed as they had done in 1600. During the Napoleonic wars, when the Dutch East India Company had not been able to send its vessels to the Indian Ocean, it had chartered American ships each year for its Japan trade, and these ships had visited Nagasaki flying the colors of the Netherlands. As their "privilege," the American sea captains brought home Japanese bronzes, lacquered boxes, and furniture produced by Nagasaki artisans for the Dutch trade. From about 1807 until 1845, however, no American ship had put in at any Japanese port. Shipwrecked American sailors were poorly treated and if they ever reached home, it was only through the good offices of the Dutch at Nagasaki. The Japanese did not even permit repatriation of their own castaways. In 1845, however, the whaling ship *Manhattan* out of Sag Harbor rescued twenty-two sailors from a shipwrecked Japanese junk and was permitted to land them at Uraga, at the entrance to Edo Bay, which eight years earlier had opened fire on the ship *Morrison* sent from Canton to repatriate seven castaways. The *Manhattan* was permitted to take on provisions at Uraga, and the incident encouraged the Americans to believe that the Japanese might be receptive to opening relations. But when Commodore James Biddle anchored off Uraga in 1846 with a letter to the shogun from President Polk, the shogun's senior councilor, Masahiro Abe, refused to accept the letter and gave instructions that the American ships be ordered to depart Japanese waters.

Commodore Perry carried a letter to the shogun from former

President Millard Fillmore, who had dispatched Perry's small squadron before the 1852 elections (in which Franklin Pierce defeated Winfield Scott). Perry, whose daughter Caroline was married to the New York millionaire August Belmont, arrived by way of Shanghai and Okinawa aboard the flagship U.S.S. *Susquehanna* and five other vessels. All foreign vessels were *kurofune* (black ships) to the Japanese, and Perry's squadron is still known in Japanese history as the Black Ships. The presidential letter that Perry carried requested a treaty, and the commodore demanded such a treaty, "as a right, and not...as a favor," saying that he would return the following spring for a favorable reply.

Commodore Perry's two steam-powered men-of-war, which had sails to supplement their paddlewheels, were the first steamships ever seen in Japan. Their arrival produced consternation at Edo, but nobody dared tell the Tokugawa shogun Ieyoshi what was happening. The shogun was ill and feeble; his senior councilor Masuhiro Abe was running the government, and when Ieyoshi did hear about the American squadron a few days later, it was only accidentally while attending a *noh* play at Edo Castle. The news upset him so much that he took to his bed and remained there until his death.

When Perry returned in February 1854 with ten ships and two thousand men, it took six weeks of negotiation before Ieyoshi's number four son Iesada, who had become shogun following the death of Ieyoshi, opened up two ports — Shimoda and Hakodate (in Hokkaido) — to American ships for supply of "wood, water, provisions and coal, and other articles their necessities may require, as far as the Japanese have them" under terms of the Treaty of Kanagawa signed March 31, 1854. What the Americans really wanted was to trade with the Japanese. The Treaty of Kanagawa did not provide that. Townsend Harris, a New York merchant who had met Commodore Perry in Hong Kong and had tried unsuccessfully to join his expedition, was the man who negotiated a commercial treaty several years later.

Harris had been trading with the Far East for some time when President Pierce appointed him consul-general to Japan in August 1855 and charged him with obtaining a commercial treaty. Harris stopped in Siam on the way to negotiate a new commercial treaty there, and by the time he arrived off Shimoda, the *daimyo* who had the most influence at Edo were not receptive to foreigners. Harris nevertheless persuaded local authorities to let him have the Gyokusen temple for his residence and raised an American flag at Shimoda. For eighteen months, Harris was left alone, ignored both by his own government and snubbed by the Tokugawa government until he was able, by tact and persistence, to negotiate a convention giving the United States the right to appoint consuls at Shimoda and Hakodate, with extra-territorial rights in each place. He also established a favorable exchange rate. Then, still without a commercial treaty, he played upon fears that European imperialists might do in Japan what they had done in China. Finally, the xenophobes lost influence at Edo, and Harris, who had learned from Perry the value of ceremony, mounted a cavalcade worthy of a *daimyo* and proceeded from Shimoda to Edo with an escort of more than three hundred and fifty persons, on horse and on foot. Riding mostly on horseback but accompanied by an oversized palanquin that he had built for himself and which required twelve bearers, Harris journeyed for eight days with the populace kowtowing before him and his retainers along the way. He entered Edo on the last day of November 1857 — the first foreign diplomat ever to be received by a shogun. He presented a letter from President Buchanan, and he demonstrated that a treaty with the United States could be had on favorable terms and would provide a buffer against the unbridled rapacity of the other Western powers.

There followed months of negotiations, during which time a plot to assassinate Harris was frustrated, and the commercial treaty was finally signed at the end of July 1858 aboard Commodore Perry's old flagship the U.S.S. *Mississippi*. Harris was fifty-one when he arrived at Shimoda and his journals dwell at length on his dyspepsia. Fascinated by the *gaijin* (foreigner), the people spied on him. For company, he had a Dutch interpreter and, according to local tradition, he also had a seventeen-year-old geisha *companion* named Okichi. The "romance" between the consul and the *geisha* is a favorite subject in popular Japanese literature and theater; whether any such liaison ever existed is questionable.

70.   Japan passed Sweden in 1977 to become the country with the world's highest life-expectancy. Life expectancy for Japanese men is 72.7 years and for women 77.9 *years. According to the Guinness Book of*

World Records, reports of people living to an age of one hundred and twenty and up in places like Hunza, Soviet Georgia, and the Ecuadorean village of Villacabamba, have never been adequately substantiated. Nobody thus far in history, says the *Guinness Book*, has lived longer than Shigechiyo Izumi of Tokunoshima, Kagoshima Prefecture, who was born in 1865 and died on his one hundred and fourteenth birthday June 29, 1979.

In the United States, white men have a life expectancy of 70.2 years, white women of 77.8 years (1978 figures). For non-whites, the rates are sixty-five and 73.6, respectively. Since women have greater life expectancy than men, it is argued that life insurance companies should charge lower premiums on policies issued to women, just as automobile insurance companies do, instead of having women's premiums subsidizing policies issued on men, just as healthy people's premiums subsidize policies issued on overweight, alcoholic, chain-smoking lion tamers.

Cardio-vascular disease is still far and away the leading cause of death in the United States, although the rate has been declining. Heart diseases are second, cancer third (with lung cancer increasing while all other kinds of cancer decrease), cerebral stroke is a distant fourth, pneumonia and influenza fifth, accidents close behind, diabetes seventh, infant mortality eighth, neonatal mortality ninth, nephritis and nephrosis tenth. Cerebral stroke is the leading cause of death in Japan, according to the Minstry of Health; it took 170,029 lives in 1977. Second is cancer (145,772 deaths in 1977); third is heart disease (103,564); fourth, pneumonia and other lung infections (32,430); fifth, accidents (30,352); sixth, natural death from old age (28,381); seventh, suicide (20,269); eighth, high blood pressure (19,333); ninth, liver diseases (15,453); and tenth, diabetes (9,509). Stomach cancer, rare in the United States, is the leading form of cancer in Japan, and this has been ascribed variously to the talc-like powder coating of polished rice and to the high Japanese consumption of spicy pickled products. Nobody really knows. The typical Japanese dinner of salt-grilled fish with soy sauce, soup, pickled radish, rice, spinach salad, strawberries, and tea has a sodium content of 4,352 milligrams; whereas a typical American dinner of roast chicken, mashed potatoes and gravy, peas, bread and butter, with apple pie and coffee has a sodium content of 1,768 milligrams. The difference probably explains why so many Japanese have high blood pressure. Japan's relatively low rate of cardiovascular disease has been related to diets low in saturated fats. Meat and butterfat consumption is extremely low in Japan. When Japanese in Hawaii and the United States shift their dietary habits to Western eating patterns, their rates of cardiovascular disease increases to approximate those of Westerners.

71.   According to the 1981 Japanese government survey, nine hundred and ten thousand people over age sixty-five were living by themselves, and seven hundred and twenty thousand of these were women. Among people over age sixty, fifty-nine per cent lived with their children or grandchildren as compared with only twelve percent in France, seven percent in the United States, and six percent in Britain.

72.   When a Japanese husband refers to his wife he uses the word *tsuma*. When a wife refers to her husband, she usually uses the word *shujin*, meaning "master." She may also call him *otto* (but not *ottō-san*), a word derived from the older word *tsuma* which, like *tsureai* (meaning "companion") was once used for both husbands and wives. A husband may refer to his *nyobo*, a word that comes from a room in the Imperial Palace used by ladies in waiting to the emperor or empress, or he may refer to her as the *kanai*, a word that means "inside of house" because a wife was expected to remain in the house most of the time. When you refer to someone else's wife in Japan, you use the word *okusan*, which comes from *okugata*. The wife of a *daimyo* in feudal Japan was an *okugata* because she stayed far in the interior of the house, the *okunoma*. In more formal circumstances, you may use the word *fujin*, meaning "Mrs." The word comes from China and was applied to the wife of a nobleman or the mistress of the emperor. Even when you know a woman quite well you do not generally call her by name, so a Japanese woman remains rather an abstract figure.

The real problem about language with respect to equality between the sexes, however, is that there are special ways for women to speak, and this affects the way women think. A woman must use feminine ways of speaking that men do not use. Because of this language difference, men in Japan do not speak to women on the same level. Men command, women entreat. To someone on his level or in a lower position, a Japanese man says, "*Suwarinasai*," meaning, "sit down," and he would use that term in speaking to his wife. To someone in a higher position, he would say, "*O-suwarikudasai*," or "Won't you please sit down." A woman would say, "*Suwarinasai*" only to a child or a servant. The words "*anata*" and "*omae*" both mean "you," but "*anata*" is more polite. A wife uses *anata* when speaking to her husband, a husband uses *omae* when speaking to his wife, who never says "*omae*" unless she says "*omae-san*".

INDEX

labor unions, 23, 75, 183
language, written, 151–153, 207
Lebra, Taki Sugiyama, 21
Lecky, William, 145
lifetime employment, 195
literacy, 29
longevity, 211–213

MacArthur, Gen. Douglas,
   134, 188, 192
Mainichi Shimbun, 98, 131, 147
marriage, 18, 42, 90, 137–139,
   157–160, 167, 187
Marubeni Corp., 45, 186
maternity leave, 72, 73, 200
Matsushita, Konosuke, 101,
   204
Matsuya, 77
medals, 7, 139, 140
medical schools, 95, 96
Meiji period, 40, 94, 165, 176,
   188, 201, 202
Meiji Shrine, 30, 165
Menard cosmetics, 105
menstrual leave, 10
mercury poisoning, 171, 172
Minamata disease, 171, 172
Mitsubishi, 45
Mitsukoshi, 9
Mitsui, 45, 73
mountain climbing, 56, 57,
   118–121
Ms. magazine, 71, 197, 198
Murakami, Yasuo, 47

Nagasaki, 32, 91, 208, 209
Nagoya, 79
Nakane, Chie, 187
nakaudo, 28, 157, 159, 160
Nara, 33, 88, 169, 206
narcotics, 155

Natsugi, 57
New Year's, 30, 79, 83, 161
NHK, 30, 207
Nichibei Fujinkai, 207, 208
Nissan, 2, 43, 76, 172
Nobunaga, Oda, 91
Noevir cosmetics, 39, 45, 46,
   51, 52, 56–60, 62–66, 69, 70,
   99–101, 126, 127
nuclear arms, 114
nuclear energy, 114, 115

Office Ladies, 182, 183
o-hashi (*see hashi*)
Okura, Hiroshi, 46–60, 62–66,
   70, 100–104, 121, 124–126,
   131
Omiya City, 2, 80, 102, 115
Onnadaigaku, 135, 136
Ozaki, Robert S., 3

pachinko, 6, 139
Pankhurst, Emmeline, 176
P.T.A., 16, 38, 86, 92, 202
parks, 9, 13–15
Paul, Alice, 176
Perry, Commodore, 191, 209,
   210
Pola cosmetics, 52, 105
police, 26, 153
pollution, 93, 170–172
population, 11, 148, 149, 154
postal service, 173
pronunciation, 172, 173
prostitution, 40, 102, 136, 174–
   176
publishing, 29, 164

quality control, 192–197
quality of life, 149